TIN TO TABLE

FANCY, SNACKY RECIPES FOR TIN-THUSIASTS AND A-FISH-IONADOS

ANNA HEZEL

Photography by Chelsie Craig
Illustrations by Alex Citrin

CHRONICLE BOOKS
SAN FRANCISCO

Library of Congress Cataloging-in-Publication Data

Names: Hezel, Anna, author. | Craig, Chelsie, photographer. | Citrin, Alex, illustrator.
Title: Tin to table : fancy, snacky recipes for tin-thusiasts and a-fish-ionados / Anna Hezel ; photography by Chelsie Craig ; illustrations by Alex Citrin.
Identifiers: LCCN 2022048430 | ISBN 9781797215518 (hardcover)
Subjects: LCSH: Cooking (Canned foods) | Cooking (Seafood) | LCGFT: Cookbooks.
Classification: LCC TX821 .H49 2023 | DDC 641.6/12--dc23/eng/20221024
LC record available at https://lccn.loc.gov/2022048430

Manufactured in China.

Photographs by **CHELSIE CRAIG**.
Food styling by **MAGGIE RUGGIERO**.
Prop styling by **SELENA LIU**.

Cover photo by **ANTONIS ACHILLEOS**.
Cover food styling by **ALI RAMEE**.

Illustration by **ALEX CITRIN**.
Design by **LIZZIE VAUGHAN**.
Typesetting by **FRANK BRAYTON**.

Typeset in Brush Crush, Harriet Text, Trade Gothic, and RB Bubble Flight.

10 9 8 7 6 5

Chronicle books and gifts are available at special quantity discounts to corporations, professional associations, literacy programs, and other organizations. For details and discount information, please contact our premiums department at corporatesales@chroniclebooks.com or at 1-800-759-0190.

Chronicle Books LLC
680 Second Street
San Francisco, California 94107
www.chroniclebooks.com

To Dan

There's no one I'd rather share a tin with.

INTRODUCTION

Which aisle of the grocery store can transport you to the cerulean coves of the Costa Brava, the rocky shores of Brittany, or the salmon smokehouses overlooking Alaska's Bristol Bay? Only the canned fish aisle, where you'll find tins full of salty treasures from around the world, miraculously preserved, sometimes mere hours after being plucked from the sea.

These tidy stacks of cans are what make the tuna melts of your late-night diner dreams come true. They're the briny anchovies that make the world of restaurant Caesar salads and bagna caudas go round. They're the juicy fried dace with salted black beans from China's Pearl River Delta, which will make your stir-fries come alive. And they're the rectangular tins of sardines that make you feel like you're picnicking on the Mediterranean, even when you're just taking a snack break in the middle of a long hike or an eight-hour workday.

The story of canned fish starts, believe it or not, with Napoleon. In 1795, facing the challenges of leading (and feeding) his troops across land and sea during the Napoleonic Wars, Napoleon offered a cash prize of 12,000 francs to the first person who invented a new method of food preservation. A chef and brewer named Nicolas Appert rose to the challenge and spent the next fourteen years figuring out how to preserve prepared foods by heating them inside glass jars and sealing these jars against any intruding microbes. A year later, in 1810, a British businessman named Peter Durand patented a similar process using tin, and canning was off to the races, ready to feed soldiers, explorers, and inlanders with a taste for oysters.

In the intervening centuries, these tins have made their way into hundreds of dishes and cuisines around the world. They've fueled overseas voyages and treks up Mount Everest. Before there was refrigeration, preserving sea creatures with plenty of salt and oil, and then vacuum sealing them in tin cans to remove oxygen, made it possible for us to enjoy them for months, years, and sometimes even decades (really, it's been done!) after they were fished out of the ocean.

A few centuries (and grocery delivery apps) later, these canned goods aren't just a pragmatic form of survival or convenience—they're luxury imports, collectibles, and souvenirs. (Who needs an album of vacation snapshots when you can just sit down with friends and show them the tins you brought back?) There are entire YouTube channels, Instagram accounts, lines of merch, and subreddits dedicated to the topic of tinned fish. We don't eat canned fish because we have to—we eat it because it's a lifestyle.

Following Spain and Portugal's lead, a whole wave of bars and restaurants in the United States have added tins to their menus, putting as much thought and care into curating their selections as they put into their wine lists. At the end of a busy day in Manhattan, you can stop at Maiden Lane for a martini and a breathtaking tin of Don Bocarte anchovies. If you're biking your way around Portland, Maine, on a warm summer day, you can drop in at the Shop (an outpost of Island Creek Oysters) for a Bloody Mary and a tin of Ramón Peña sardines, served with a smattering of great pickles and slices of honey wheat bread. There's Saltie Girl, in Boston; Bar Diane, in Portland, Oregon; and JarrBar, in Seattle. This is only a small sampling of the many restaurants that are putting their own personalized stamps on curated selections of tins.

Ironically, just as many of us became comfortable with the idea of tinned fish as a luxury product, it unexpectedly became a pragmatic means of survival again. In the spring of 2020, when COVID-19 started to transform our shopping and eating habits, we stocked up on the shelf-stable foods that would tide us over between trips to the grocery store, which felt increasingly perilous. In my neighborhood in Brooklyn, New York, a number of restaurants turned their out-of-commission dining rooms into impromptu grocery markets. And almost every one included a tinned fish section.

Every producer, importer, and cannery I spoke to over the course of writing this book noticed a sudden spike in interest during those early months of the pandemic. People were stuck at home cooking for themselves, and tinned seafood was a silver bullet: delicious, easy to prepare, and healthful. There were enough different types and styles of canned seafood that you could open a new tin every night of the year without ever eating the same thing twice, as you traveled from one ocean to another from the comfort of home.

As more and more home cooks and their families cut down on their meat consumption out of concern for the environment, canned fish offers a happy alternative, packed full of protein and omega-3s. And in an age of conscious consumerism, canned seafood can offer transparency about sourcing, fishing methods, sustainability, and mercury levels, which can be difficult or impossible to trace among the fresh seafood at the supermarket or on a restaurant menu.

The convergence of all of these factors has reshaped the canning industry in refreshing new ways. Home cooks' growing passion for small-scale, quality products has encouraged a whole new generation of independent producers to enter the scene. Güeyu Mar, a restaurant in Asturias, Spain, started to package and sell their char-grilled seafoods in 2017. Three years later, their eye-catching paper-wrapped cans reached the US market, where they quickly became a fixture, from the pages of *Bon Appétit* to the shelves of specialty food stores.

In late 2020, Caroline Goldfarb and Becca Millstein launched Fishwife with a modest online store of two products— a smoked wild salmon and a smoked albacore tuna. In mere months, the Los Angeles–based brand became a household name. In 2021, chef and former *Top Chef* contestant Sara Hauman launched the Tiny Fish Co. with a line of products highlighting some of the Pacific Northwest's most sustainable species, like mussels, rockfish, and geoduck.

There's never been a more exciting or auspicious time to eat tinned seafood. While it might be tempting to call it a trend, I think of it more as an art form that's still being forged and perfected, several centuries in. My greatest hope for this book is that avid tin collectors and tinned seafood converts alike will find new ways of cooking with and appreciating these familiar ingredients. The world is very big and full of tins. Let's crack open a few together. ■

A FIELD GUIDE TO TINNED SEAFOOD

It's easy to become overwhelmed by microscopic choices when you're starting to build a collection of tinned seafood, or even if you're curious to try a species you've never had before. Canola oil or olive? Packed with piri-piri peppers or miso? Skin-on or filleted? With millions of products out there (and many claiming to be "gourmet"), where should a fish enthusiast even begin?

This guide is a brief introduction to the seafood you'll encounter most frequently in this book. The recommended tins below are by no means the best ones money can buy— they're just products that I've tried, enjoyed, and would heartily recommend to friends. Many recipes in this book suggest brands that are well suited to a particular dish. But it would be a shame to let your tinned seafood journey end with these recommendations. If a tin of Agromar scorpionfish pâté, Ekone smoked oysters, Donostia scallops, or Old Fisherman eel catches your eye, buy it! Have some friends over for a tasting party, or consider sharing your thoughts with some fellow a-fish-ionados and tin-thusiasts over on the r/CannedSardines subreddit.

anchovies

1. CODESA SERIE ORO (GOLD SERIES) ANCHOVIES IN OLIVE OIL

Like ribbons of mature Parmesan or thin slices of aged prosciutto, these are snackable right out of the tin.

2. ORTIZ GRAN SELECCIÓN ANCHOVIES IN OLIVE OIL

These have a mild flavor (in the universe of anchovies) and a firm texture, which make them perfect for wrapping around an olive to create Gildas (page 96).

3. YURRITA ANCHOVIES IN OLIVE OIL

These clean-tasting anchovies are perfect for bagna cauda or Caesar dressing.

Unlike many tinned seafoods, anchovies are generally sold in a partially preserved form: They've been coated in salt while raw, aged for about six months, and then cleaned, filleted, and packed in olive oil. This means two things. First of all, unlike sardines, which are generally fully cooked and can last for years in the tin, you should use anchovies within about a year of buying them. This also means that anchovies are more temperature-sensitive than other canned products. It's a good idea to keep them in a cool, dark place—ideally the refrigerator.

Once the fillets are past their prime, or have been stored in a warm environment, they can become brown and mushy—a far cry from the beautiful pink ribbons they resemble when fresh. If you've only ever had brown, mushy anchovies, it's not your fault (or the anchovies' fault). A lot of grocery stores just don't keep them cold enough or turn over product quickly enough.

Treat yourself to a tin of Ortiz, Arroyabe, Codesa, or even the ultraluxurious Don Bocarte variety, and you'll be shocked by the difference. You can also buy anchovies packed in salt from brands like Agostina Recca and clean and fillet them yourself (see page 176).

clams and cockles

THREE TINS TO TRY

1. CONSERVAS DE CAMBADOS MEDIUM CLAMS

Juicy and delicate, these are great for snacking alongside some ripe tomato slices on a summer day.

2. DONOSTIA COCKLES IN BRINE

These have a bright, mineral flavor and a balanced salinity, which make them perfect bites between sips of martini.

3. GÜEYU MAR CHAR-GRILLED RAZOR CLAMS

Razor clams tend to be slightly meatier and heartier than other varieties of clams, which is why they complement the soft smoke of a grill.

A really good can of clams or cockles (which are smaller and more tender than clams) delivers a clean, mineral, almost sweet taste of the ocean in every bite. Those bites might even taste fresher than some fresh clams you've eaten in your life. You may be tempted to drink the brine. (And you should! More on that under Wait, Don't Throw Out the Brine! on page 86.)

But much like tuna and salmon, their grocery-store-shelf pals, clams can vary wildly in quality depending on whether you're buying a large-scale, industrial, machine-processed can or a beautiful artisanal can that was hand-packed in Galicia. And while the grocery store can of minced or chopped clams is great for an improvised linguine with clam sauce or a batch of Canned Clam Garlic Bread (page 83), if you're going to pop open a can to snack on, look for the tins that are hand-packed in brine from brands like Matiz, Donostia, Cabo de Peñas, Ramón Peña, Espinaler, or Bogar.

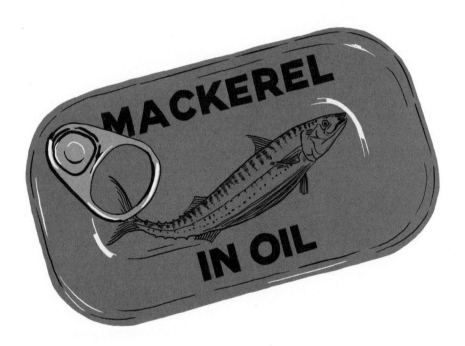

mackerel

I. CONSERVAS SANTOS MEDITERRANEAN-STYLE MACKEREL FILLETS

A perfect, clean-tasting mackerel to incorporate in a salad or pack into a sandwich.

2. MINERVA MACKEREL FILLETS IN SPICED OLIVE OIL WITH PICKLES

This would be my "stranded on a desert island" tin of choice—rich, meaty fillets mildly spiced with piri-piri pepper and gently sweetened by a single carrot slice and a pickle slice.

3. PATAGONIA PROVISIONS SMOKED MACKEREL IN OLIVE OIL

This mackerel has just a subtle whisper of smoke and is versatile enough to eat with some crackers and hot sauce, or in a carefully composed rice bowl.

The term *mackerel* is applied to many different species of fish that have certain physical and nutritional qualities in common, much like anchovies and sardines. And like anchovies and sardines, the flavor of the meat relies heavily on what liquid the fish is packed in, which is why I always look for olive oil on the label. Some smaller species of mackerel are packaged intact, with skin on and bones in. Usually labeled "small mackerel," they are similar in taste to sardines, but with a firmer texture and smoother skin.

Larger mackerel species are often canned as skinless, boneless fillets, which resemble the meaty flakiness of tuna, and can actually be a great (and in many cases, more sustainable) substitution for it. These are usually labeled "mackerel fillets" or just "mackerel." Sometimes the fish is smoked before it goes into the can, and sometimes it's packed with pickles, spicy chiles, or slices of lemon.

If you're a tinned fish eater, there's probably a perfect mackerel out there, just waiting for you to find it. Maybe it's an easygoing tin of Patagonia smoked mackerel, packed with paprika, or some buttery Minerva fillets in olive oil.

mussels

I. MATIZ ORGANIC MUSSELS IN OLIVE OIL AND VINEGAR

These are brilliantly acidic, glossy beauties.

2. PALACIO DE ORIENTE MUSSELS IN SPICY PICKLED SAUCE

These are packed in an escabeche sauce full of paprika and garlic.

3. PATAGONIA PROVISIONS SMOKED MUSSELS IN OLIVE OIL AND BROTH

A smoky twist on the usual tinned mussel template, swapping out the vinaigrette for a savory broth.

To me, mussels are the underrated jewels of the tinned seafood world. In contrast to the mussels in the shell you might buy to steam or cook into a spicy marinara, tinned mussels have a tender, almost buttery mouthfeel, with none of the elasticity (or sometimes rubbery texture) of their fresh counterparts.

A very common preparation for Spanish mussels is to pack the bivalves in escabeche sauce (sometimes labeled "pickled sauce" or "olive oil and vinegar"), which is bright with vinegar and often tinged with warm spices like paprika, cloves, and nutmeg. You also might come across mussels that have been smoked or packed in a whole array of different sauces and flavorings, which are intended to be enjoyed straight out of the can.

Not only are these mollusks packed with protein, vitamin B_{12}, and iron—they also reproduce quickly and improve the water quality within their aquaculture ecosystems. These little guys are heroes of the ocean and of the party.

octopus

THREE TINS TO TRY

I. CONSERVAS DE CAMBADOS OCTOPUS IN GALICIAN SAUCE

These tentacles are packed in Galician sauce, which brings together sweet onion with warming, vivid-orange paprika.

2. MATIZ OCTOPUS IN OLIVE OIL

A great economical choice for octopus that's deeply savory and ready to be turned into a tapa or salad.

3. RAMÓN PEÑA OCTOPUS IN OLIVE OIL

The segments of this octopus are beautifully arranged in the tin and ready to be speared with toothpicks, making this tin a worthwhile splurge when presentation matters.

If I'm being completely honest, one reason I'm so attached to canned octopus is my fear of cooking fresh octopus, which can be expensive, intimidating, and extremely easy to mess up. But when I spend a few dollars on a favorite can of octopus, I can rest easy knowing that the cannery probably got it right.

Canned octopus can be just as fancy as its fresh counterpart at a restaurant, but you can serve it with far less stress, whether you're tossing the tentacle pieces with crunchy cucumbers and herbs for a summery salad, or setting out the tin with a cup of toothpicks for a party snack. The meat is surprisingly absorbent toward neighboring flavors, so definitely opt for something packed in good-quality olive oil. I like to warm the octopus slightly in olive oil before serving, which I do when making Octopus Marinated with Chili Powder & Orange Peel (page 115).

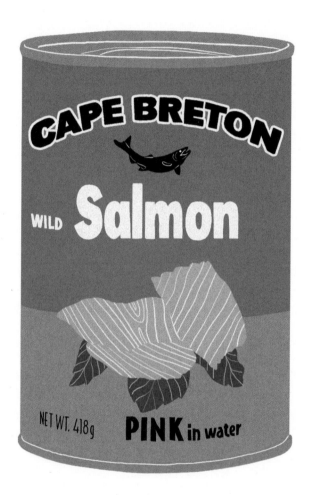

salmon

THREE TINS TO TRY

I. FISHWIFE SMOKED ATLANTIC SALMON

Tender and slightly sweetened by brown sugar, this one is great on toast or flaked into steamed rice.

2. SCOUT SMOKED WILD PINK SALMON

A mild, gently smoked choice for folding into scrambled eggs or frittatas.

3. WILDFISH CANNERY SMOKED KING SALMON

This tin has a robustly smoky flavor that brings out all the best qualities in this wild-caught Alaskan king salmon.

The salmon canning industry has existed in the United States since the mid-1800s, and many succeeding generations of Americans got their first taste of the fish straight from the can. Canned salmon is still one of the most common tinned seafood products you'll find in an American grocery store. Because so many of the canned salmon in North America have been caught wild in Alaska, where local regulations are designed to keep salmon populations thriving, these products also tend to be very sustainable.

While a lot of the offerings come from large-scale, industrial canneries, there are a few independent companies, like Wildfish Cannery, Scout, and Fishwife, selling thoughtfully crafted, beautifully smoked fillets of salmon in cans. This is not the 1960s casserole ingredient of yore; it's a product you'll be tempted to toss over freshly steamed rice or eat straight from the can with a cold beer.

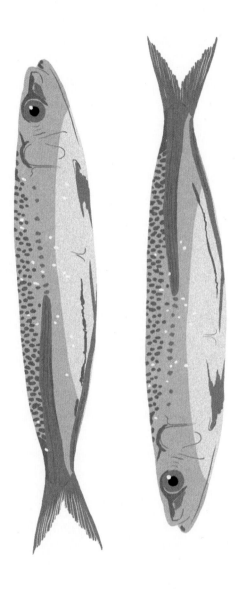

sardines

THREE TINS TO TRY

1. ESPINALER BABY SARDINES IN OLIVE OIL

Dainty little mild-flavored sardines, which are perfect for cocktail-hour snacking.

2. NURI SPICED SARDINES IN OLIVE OIL

These meaty sardines are bathed in a silky orange oil that's packed with warm aromatic flavors, like piri-piri peppers and cloves.

3. PINHAIS SARDINES IN TOMATO SAUCE

These are packed in a bright, acidic tomato sauce, which you could easily heat up in a skillet and toss with pasta.

I am almost always in the mood for sardines. These fatty, flavorful little fish taste equally satisfying as a hurried meal when you're ravenous after a long run, or as the accompaniment to a champagne toast. They can act as the meaty filling for a spicy cilantro and pickle–packed banh mi, or as the salty taste of the sea in a dish of garlicky bucatini with lots of caramelized fennel.

While you can definitely find skinless, boneless fillets, the skin and bones in these fish are packed with nutrients. They're also part of the aesthetic experience. When you peel back the lid of a can, you see the handiwork that went into laying these silvery, tapered sardine pieces so elegantly into their packages—often mere hours after the sardines were caught.

I'm a bit of a purist when it comes to sardines and usually opt for fish that have been packed in unflavored olive oil (sometimes after being smoked or grilled for an extra layer of flavor). That being said, sardines packed with a hint of lemon or spice can be beautiful, and one of my favorite cans is Nuri Spiced Sardines in Olive Oil, which come bathed in a bright orange oil full of warm clove, bay leaf, and black pepper flavors. Many brands also sell sardines in a mellow, acidic tomato sauce, which can be a joy to sop up with bread.

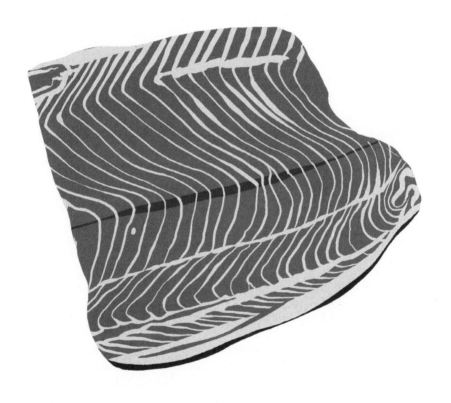

trout

1. COLE'S SMOKED RAINBOW TROUT

Tender and mild, this trout is a great choice for eating with eggs or piling onto a bagel.

2. JOSE GOURMET SMOKED TROUT FILLETS IN OLIVE OIL

These skin-on fillets look (and taste) delightfully fresh, as if they've just emerged from a bustling restaurant kitchen.

3. TRADER JOE'S FARM RAISED SMOKED TROUT IN CANOLA OIL

For an unbeatable price, this tin will bring a heavy-duty dose of salt and smoke to your next salad.

Much like salmon, most of the canned trout I buy is smoked. The intensely salty, woodsy taste can add a baconlike note of indulgence to a salad or a batch of lentils marinated in vinaigrette. But to truly spotlight its flavor, I like to flake the fish into a mix of crème fraîche and cream cheese and use it as a dip for potato chips (see the Smoked Trout Dip, page 71).

There are some great inexpensive cans out there (I always have some Trader Joe's trout around). But to me, the real mark of quality is a delicate, tender texture, which is why I'll occasionally spend a few extra dollars for a JOSE Gourmet can.

tuna

THREE TINS TO TRY

1. OLASAGASTI VENTRESCA DE ATUN CLARO (YELLOWFIN TUNA BELLY)

A luxuriously fatty cut, ideal for snacking on straight from the tin with some harissa and olives.

2. ORTIZ BONITO DEL NORTE (NORTHERN TUNA)

A meaty, flavorful standby for composed salads.

3. SEA TALES SOLID WHITE ALBACORE WILD TUNA IN OLIVE OIL (OR IN WATER)

A mild but delicious option for sandwiches and melts.

There's nothing quite like the nostalgia of a toasty, melty, diner-style tuna melt or a creamy, golden-top tuna noodle casserole. This may be why canned tuna is one of America's favorite seafoods. Unfortunately, tuna's mass popularity, combined with the fact that tuna are predators with crucial roles in the ocean ecosystem, means that overfishing has colossal environmental repercussions. This is why I think of tuna less as a routine source of protein and more as an occasional treat that's worth sourcing thoughtfully.

As a guiding principle, look for tuna that's been caught by pole and line—a technique that minimizes both bycatch and pollution. If you're planning to eat the fish right out of the can, definitely opt for something packed in olive oil. But if you'll be mixing the tuna with plenty of mayo for a sandwich, or béchamel sauce for a casserole, water-packed is a great choice.

THE TINNED FISH PANTRY

I'll never forget traveling to the Costa Brava in Spain for the first time and drinking a vermouth on the beach while watching the sunset at Boia Nit, a cocktail bar in Cadaqués. I ordered a tin of cockles, which was served with just a drizzle of sherry vinegar, a few grinds of black pepper, and a proportionately small bowl of potato sticks. I was blown away by how much an assemblage of pantry ingredients could bring out the clean, fresh taste of the cockles.

It may seem counterintuitive to order canned fish at a restaurant when it's so cheap and easy to eat at home. But when I see the tin list on the menu, I can't help myself. Even when there's a slight price markup from the seven or eight dollars that the tin might cost at the grocery store, I am always curious to see how the restaurant will put its own twist on the tin. You could order a tin of Ramón Peña sardines at five different restaurants, and each experience might be wildly different.

Sometimes tinned fish is accompanied by freshly made bread and a complex compound butter, and other times by an exciting array of pickles, mustard, and hot sauces. Here are a few of the pantry ingredients I like to keep around to make my tins shine a little brighter when I'm feeling fancy.

CHILI CRISP • Chili crisp is a real heavy-lifter condiment in my household, where the ruby-colored oil—often packed with some combination of Sichuan peppercorns, fermented black beans, alliums, garlic, and sesame seeds—adds salty heat and crunch to dumpling sauces, bowls of soup, and fried rice. It can also add dimension to a tin of oil-packed sardines or a smoked salmon rice bowl. I love to make it at home, but you can't go wrong with a jar of Lao Gan Ma or Fly By Jing.

CHIPS • There are almost always potato chips in my apartment, whether that means an iconic blue-and-white canister of Bonilla a la Vista or a bag of Zapp's Voodoo chips. The fried texture is a perfect accompaniment to the less fatty tinned seafoods, like clams, mussels, cockles, and octopus.

CRACKERS • Canned fish proselytizers, myself included, tend to sound like a broken record when it comes to recommending pairing canned fish with bread and butter. But there's nothing quite like the retro charm of a stack of saltines or Triscuits, especially when you're feeding a crowd.

HARISSA • A good harissa can deliver a powerful dose of fruity chile flavor and coriander, which brings warmth to tuna sandwiches, snack plates with sardines and olives, and mixed platters like S'han Tounsi with Mokli (page 130). I'm an especially big fan of the harissa made by Zwïta, which comes in mild, spicy, and smoky.

HOT SAUCE • Smoked seafood, like oysters, mussels, and mackerel, can gain a lot from a few shakes of a really bright and peppery hot sauce. As someone who grew up in Buffalo, I'm partial to Frank's RedHot, an essential ingredient of buffalo wings, but I can also get behind Tabasco. The Spanish company Espinaler makes an "appetizer sauce," which delivers a heady dose of paprika and vinegar and is great sprinkled over mussels and potato chips, like the Vermouth Hour Potato Chips with Mussels, Olives & Piparras (page 116).

MUSTARD • A long-standing menu item at Prune, Gabrielle Hamilton's restaurant in Manhattan, consisted of a can of sardines, a stack of Triscuits, a spoonful of Dijon mustard, and a pile of cornichons. Paired with a luxuriously oily fish, mustard offers an acidic, peppery reprieve from the richness, just as it does alongside pâté or chicken liver mousse. I'm a fan of Maille, which you can buy in a classic Dijon style or in a whole-grain form.

PICKLES • I've never regretted having an extra jar of pickles in the cupboard, especially when a party spread calls for something crunchy and refreshing. To eat with canned fish, I highly recommend Matiz or Donostia brand piparras (pickled guindilla peppers), Maille cornichons, and McClure's spicy spears.

VINEGAR • I like to keep at least three vinegars in my kitchen: a mild wine or champagne vinegar for vinaigrettes, a subtly sweet aged sherry vinegar to drizzle over tinned clams or cockles, and a malt vinegar, which tastes great with fried foods, like Fish & Chips for One (page 181).

A NOTE ON SALT

Canned fish can be salty. *Really* salty. I can't tell you how many times I've set out to cook something with tinned fish, adding my usual pinch of salt here and another one there, only to reach the end and realize that I've completely overdone it. What's more, a salt-cured anchovy is going to be many times saltier than an oil-packed sardine, and every brand and product is slightly different.

This is why many of the recipes in this book use a cautious hand when salting. I still like to salt the water I use for cooking pasta or lentils, or for blanching vegetables (I like Diamond Crystal salt, because it's significantly less salty than other brands of kosher salt). But in general, it's a good idea to wait until after you've added the tinned fish to taste a dish for seasoning. Sometimes you won't need to add any salt at all, and other times you might decide on just a light sprinkle of flaky Maldon or Jacobsen sea salt for crunch.

HOW TO STORE YOUR TINNED FISH

Following the lead of many of the producers, chefs, and specialty grocers I've consulted over the years, I refrigerate all of my anchovies, and I eat them within a year of purchase. This is because salt-cured anchovies are a partially preserved product, and their quality can degrade over time—a process that is expedited if they're stored at warmer temperatures.

For most other tins, just pick a place to store them where they won't be exposed to high temperatures. After transferring my own growing collection from cupboard to drawer to closet, I landed on a small, three-tier kitchen cart, which makes it easy to browse the whole array at once. If you're planning to age any of your fish or keep them for more than a year or two (oil-packed sardines are best for this treatment), store them in a cool, dry place, and rotate the tins every few months so that the contents remain coated in oil.

STRAIGHT OUT OF THE CAN

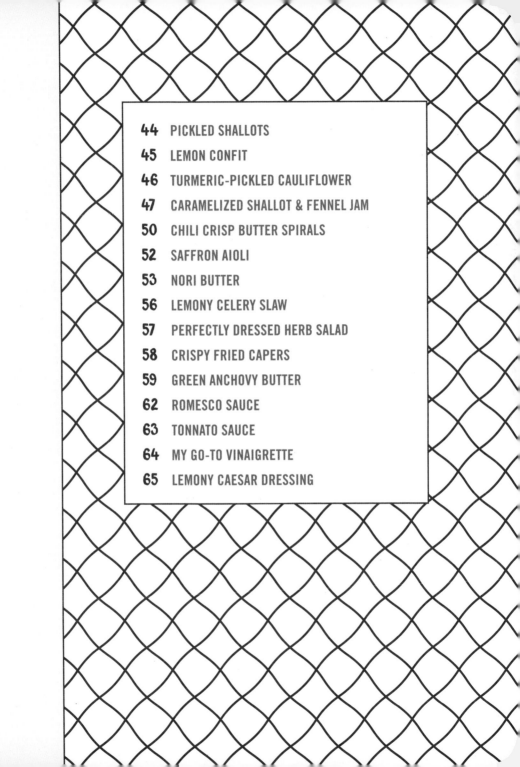

A tin that you've been saving at the back of your cupboard can be the beginning of a beautiful pasta dish or a delicate savory pastry. But part of the fun of keeping a collection of preserved seafood on hand is the instant gratification waiting for you once you pull back the metal tab. The aluminum seal is broken, and you can smell the harmonious mix of salty ocean breeze and fruity olive oil. It's one of the classiest ways I can think of to start a great party.

This is why, when I have a really special can of tender razor clams from northern Spain or a tin of sparkling silver sardines from Brittany, I like to treat them with a light touch. They're a little like that awesome thirty-year single malt in your liquor cabinet—perfect for pulling out on special occasions, but probably not the first thing you grab to make your next Scotch and soda.

The advantages of enjoying seafood straight from the can are twofold. First, it's an opportunity to appreciate the actual handiwork that went into the canning process—the way someone placed each and every cockle in a can so that the mollusks' pointy feet are all aimed upward, like the sails of tiny ships, or the way sardines are packed tail to gill to look like they've been seamlessly woven together.

It's also a way to appreciate these flavors in their purest form—exactly as they were placed in the can. This means that you're tasting the fish more or less as it tasted only a few hours after being caught, with minimal tinkering and few additional flavors beyond salt, smoke, or oil. The recipes in this chapter offer some ideas for simple condiments and accompaniments that play up these natural flavors.

In general, the tinned fish that lend themselves especially well to devouring straight from the can are the ones crafted with some of this extra care. You probably want to reach for the cans that were hand-packed (and as a result, are a little pricier), and the seafoods that have been packed in olive oil, escabeche, or brine, rather than water, canola oil, or vegetable oil. In addition to these guiding principles, here are a few tips on how to enjoy these sea creatures with minimal preparation:

ANCHOVIES • Since anchovies deliver an intense thwack of salt, they're perfect for wrapping around sweeter vegetables (think crisp sugar snap peas and juicy, fresh tomatoes) and olives with a briny, fruity taste.

SARDINES, MACKEREL, AND TUNA • These meatier fish have a much milder flavor than anchovies, and they can hold up to toast spread with smoky harissas, spicy mustards, creamy compound butters, and lots of lemon. Try them with the Lemon Confit (page 45), for example. Serve these tins with a small fork for dainty flaking, and plenty of fresh bread.

SMOKED TROUT OR SALMON • Smoked fish love a little tang, so break out the crème fraîche, pickles (such as the Pickled Shallots on page 44), capers, and a stack of saltines.

OCTOPUS • Sprinkle some minced flat-leaf parsley and a pinch of paprika right into the tin and serve with a stack of toothpicks, or add some Saffron Aioli (page 52) for dipping.

MUSSELS • Anything packed in escabeche sauce (sometimes called pickled sauce) is already seasoned in a vinegary marinade full of paprika and other spices. These are great on their own, alongside a pile of potato chips. If you have mussels packed in olive oil, give the whole can a squeeze of lemon before serving.

CLAMS • Clams, razor clams, and cockles are usually packed in a salty brine with a deep umami flavor. When you're serving these, pour off a little bit of the brine (save it for a martini or a Bloody Mary), and give the whole can a drizzle of your best sherry vinegar and a few grinds of black pepper.

WHAT DO I REALLY NEED TO KNOW ABOUT MERCURY?

It's a terrifying prospect, but most of the seafood we eat has some quantity of mercury in it. And while people all over the world eat fish daily, it's still a good idea to follow FDA recommendations, which weigh a fish's nutritional advantages (like protein and omega-3 fatty acids) with its risks.

The general FDA advice for adults is to stick to two to three 4 oz [115 g] servings of fish per week (specific advice for children and people who are pregnant or breastfeeding can be found at www.fda.gov).

The reason for this caution has to do with the fact that microorganisms in the ocean can produce methylmercury, an organic compound of mercury that can accumulate in animals and grow in concentration as it travels through the food chain. If a big fish eats a lot of tiny fish, each containing trace amounts of methylmercury, then that big fish will have a high concentration of methylmercury in its system.

This means that sea creatures that are smaller, younger, or lower on the food chain tend to have much lower mercury levels than predators like tuna, swordfish, and sharks. When it comes to tuna, certain species, like skipjack and yellowfin, tend to have lower mercury levels than others.

Personally, I think of tuna as a delicious treat for every once in a while. But on a weekly basis, I eat more tiny fish and bivalves, which are less susceptible to contamination and often have the added bonus of being more sustainable.

Pickled Shallots

These pickled minced shallots are a little like a mignonette that you might spoon over a fresh oyster. And for the same reasons that the raw, vinegary crunch complements the oyster, it will also be a great match for tinned seafood. Add a small condiment bowl of these to your next tinned fish party platter, spoon some gently over a briny tin of cockles, or mix them into a classic tuna salad. You can even use them as the foundation of a great salad dressing: Just whisk in ¼ cup [60 ml] of olive oil and 1 tsp of good Dijon mustard.

1 LARGE SHALLOT, MINCED
(ABOUT ¼ CUP [50 G])

¼ CUP [60 ML] WHITE
WINE VINEGAR

1 TBSP SUGAR

½ TSP KOSHER SALT

Makes ½ cup [110 g]   Combine the ingredients in a small jar, and mix gently to distribute and dissolve the sugar. Cover the jar and allow to marinate in the refrigerator for at least 2 hours. The shallots will keep in the refrigerator for up to 1 week.

Lemon Confit

A short, low simmer in olive oil turns a few slices of lemon into a luscious, jewel-like condiment. The confit treatment softens the bite of the citrus and brings out some of its sweeter, more floral attributes. Serve this with tinned mackerel and a stack of saltines, or toss it (olive oil and all) into some spaghetti with a tin of anchovy fillets.

1 LEMON, SLICED
⅛ IN [3 MM] THICK,
SLICES QUARTERED

½ CUP [120 ML] OLIVE OIL

1 TSP SUGAR

¼ TSP SALT

10 PEPPERCORNS

1 BAY LEAF

Makes 1 cup [200 g]   Combine all the ingredients in a small saucepan over the lowest heat possible. Cook for 20 minutes, until the lemon pieces are slightly translucent and soft enough to eat, but not mushy or falling apart. If they still have a raw, firm texture, cook for 10 minutes longer. Let cool to room temperature, and either serve immediately or transfer to a sealed container (with the olive oil and aromatics) and store in the refrigerator for up to 1 week.

Turmeric-Pickled Cauliflower

These peppery cauliflower pickles, tinted bright yellow by the turmeric, are almost a cross between two popular relishes: a fiery giardiniera and a sweet chowchow. They will add a burst of sunshine to any tinned fish snack plate and a refreshing crunch to a sandwich, like the Triple Pickle Smoked Salmon Butter Sandwich (page 150). You can also make these with romanesco broccoli for a beautiful spectrum of yellow and green.

1 SMALL HEAD CAULIFLOWER OR ROMANESCO BROCCOLI, BROKEN INTO BITE-SIZE FLORETS

4 SMALL GARLIC CLOVES

2 DRIED CHILES

1 CUP [240 ML] CIDER VINEGAR

¼ CUP [50 G] SUGAR

½ TSP KOSHER SALT

1 TSP MUSTARD SEEDS

¼ TSP TURMERIC

¼ TSP BLACK PEPPERCORNS

Makes enough to fill a 1 qt [945 ml] jar   Put the cauliflower or broccoli florets, garlic, and dried chiles in a 1 qt [945 ml] glass jar.

In a small saucepan, heat the vinegar, sugar, salt, mustard seeds, turmeric, peppercorns, and 1 cup [240 ml] of water over medium-high heat. Give the liquid a few stirs to help dissolve the salt and sugar, and bring to a vigorous boil.

Pour the liquid over the cauliflower in the jar. Let cool to room temperature, cover, and refrigerate overnight. The pickled cauliflower will keep, refrigerated, for up to 2 weeks.

Caramelized Shallot & Fennel Jam

This dark, savory jam is one of my favorite accompaniments to sardines or mackerel. A small bowl of this on a snack board can give these tiny fish a cooked-all-day flavor without sacrificing the fresh texture of fish straight from the can.

Use this jam as a building block for a composed party snack, like the Spicy Sardine Toasts with Caramelized Shallot & Fennel Jam (page 101), or even on a slapdash baguette sandwich with some oil-packed tuna. If you end up with leftovers, consider stirring them into your next frittata or a quick egg scramble with sardines.

1 SMALL FENNEL BULB OR ½ LARGE FENNEL BULB

3 TBSP OLIVE OIL

¼ TSP KOSHER SALT

2 LARGE SHALLOTS, HALVED AND THINLY SLICED

1 TBSP AGED SHERRY VINEGAR

Makes 1 cup [300 g]   Trim off the roots and stalks of the fennel and shave thinly with a mandoline, or slice thinly with a sharp knife. Heat a large skillet with a lid over high heat and add the olive oil. Add the fennel to the pan with the salt. Cook, tossing every minute or so, for 5 minutes, or until the fennel has softened and lightly browned.

Add the shallots and cook, stirring frequently, for about 3 minutes, or until the shallots have become limp and translucent. Turn the heat to low, add 1 Tbsp of water, and cover the pan. Cook for 25 minutes, stirring every 5 minutes, until the mixture has a jamlike texture. If the pan looks excessively dry at any point, just add another tablespoon of water.

Uncover, and raise the heat to high. Cook for 5 minutes, stirring constantly. Stir in the vinegar and cook until the liquid has evaporated. Serve immediately or store in a tightly covered container in the refrigerator for up to 3 days.

Chili Crisp Butter Spirals

I'm always happy when a restaurant serves bread and butter with dinner, especially when that butter is stylishly presented—pressed into individual shell-shaped medallions, shaved into curls, or sculpted into the shape of a lamb, a tradition in Buffalo around Easter. These butter spirals are like a compound butter and a party decoration rolled (literally) into one. Served with bread, they make a great, spicy accompaniment to sardines, especially when you add a bowlful of Lemony Celery Slaw (page 56). And if you've ever made slice-and-bake pinwheel cookies, you'll be a natural at the process. Chili crisp plays a lot of roles here, bringing color, heat, a garlicky flavor, and crunch, so choose one you really love. (I'm a big fan of Fly By Jing and S&B brands.) Here, you'll use the solids from the chili crisp, since the oil can throw off the texture of the butter, making your spirals fall apart.

½ CUP [113 G] SALTED BUTTER, AT ROOM TEMPERATURE

½ TSP SOLIDS FROM A JAR OF CHILI CRISP

Makes ½ cup [113 g]   Cut 1 Tbsp off the stick of butter and transfer it to a small, heatproof bowl. Add the chili crisp and microwave on high for about 30 seconds, pausing to give the mixture a stir at least once. Let cool to room temperature.

Place the rest of the stick of butter between two sheets of wax paper, about 10 in [25 cm] long. Using the bottom of a heavy metal saucepan or skillet, flatten the butter into a rectangle about 5 in [13 cm] wide and 7 in [18 cm] long. Put the butter (still between the sheets of wax paper) on a baking sheet or plate, and transfer to the freezer for 5 minutes.

Remove the butter from the freezer and remove the top layer of wax paper. With a wide spoon, spread the cooled butter–chili crisp mixture across the surface of the chilled butter, all the way to the edges. Freeze for another 5 minutes.

Check on the butter. You want it to be firm but malleable in order to create the roll. If it feels mushy, freeze for another 5 minutes. If it feels brittle, leave at room temperature for 5 minutes before proceeding.

Starting with the narrow end of the rectangle closest to you, roll the butter into a tight spiral, using the wax paper as a buffer between your hands and the butter. Roll the log up in the wax paper, and gently even it out if any spots are thicker. Refrigerate for at least 30 minutes.

When you're ready to serve, remove from the refrigerator and let come to room temperature for about 10 minutes. Give the log a few more gentle rolls back and forth on a flat surface, just to smooth out any bumpy spots. With a sharp knife, cut the log into ½ in [13 mm] spiral slices, and serve. Store any remaining spirals in a covered container in the refrigerator for up to 3 days.

Saffron Aioli

Aioli is one of those condiments that gets way too much credit for being fancy, when it takes only a few minutes and a handful of pantry ingredients to put together. And that small effort is extremely worth it when most of your meal is coming from a can. The vivid golden hue and floral muskiness of this one comes from the tiniest pinch of saffron, which goes a long way once you've steeped it in a few squeezes of lemon juice. Serve this alongside a tin of octopus packed in olive oil, some mussels in escabeche, or smoked oysters.

1 TBSP FRESH LEMON JUICE

¼ TSP DIJON MUSTARD

⅛ TSP CRUMBLED SAFFRON THREADS

⅛ TSP KOSHER SALT

1 SMALL GARLIC CLOVE, FINELY GRATED

2 EGG YOLKS, AT ROOM TEMPERATURE

½ CUP [120 ML] OLIVE OIL

Makes about ⅓ cup [80 g]   Combine the lemon juice, mustard, saffron threads, salt, and garlic in a blender (or in a jar with an immersion blender). Let sit for 10 minutes, giving a gentle shake or a stir a couple times to help distribute the salt and saffron into the liquid.

Add the egg yolks and blend on low speed until well combined. With the blender speed still on low, add the olive oil in a slow, steady stream, pausing every few seconds to make sure it's incorporated. After about a third of the olive oil has been added, you'll notice the mixture begin to emulsify and thicken.

Serve immediately, or store in a tightly covered container in the refrigerator for up to 2 days.

Nori Butter

Nori has both a minerality and a toasted warmth that can elegantly round out the flavor of fish. Combine it with some fried shallots and cultured butter (regular salted butter will also be fantastic), and you have a spread that's tangy, salty, and delightfully oceanic. This would be a great compound butter to use for basting a delicate fresh fish in a pan, but it's also the perfect complement for a snack of sourdough and sardines packed in olive oil.

1 TBSP OLIVE OIL

1 SMALL SHALLOT, THINLY SLICED

ONE 7 BY 8 IN [17 BY 20 CM] SHEET NORI

½ CUP [113 G] SALTED CULTURED BUTTER, AT ROOM TEMPERATURE

¼ TSP KOSHER SALT

Makes ½ cup [113 g] Heat the olive oil in a small skillet over medium-low heat. Add the shallot and cook, stirring occasionally, for about 7 minutes, or until golden brown and slightly shriveled. Remove from the heat and let cool to room temperature.

Meanwhile, break the sheet of nori into bite-size pieces, and use a spice grinder or clean coffee grinder to pulverize it into a powder.

In a blender (or in a jar with an immersion blender), blend together the shallot, nori powder, butter, and salt until evenly combined. Taste and add more salt as needed.

Serve immediately, or store in a tightly covered container in the refrigerator for up to 5 days.

Lemony Celery Slaw

Celery is a wildly underrated vegetable. A hardy bunch of celery will hold up in the refrigerator for a solid 2 weeks, lending its flavor, along the way, to pots of stock, mirepoix, Bloody Marys, and, of course, tuna sandwiches. And when your tinned fish plate needs something green, about 5 minutes of slicing and whisking will give you a refined celery slaw that's a perfect match for smoked sardines, ventresca (tuna belly), octopus, or whatever tin you're popping open.

½ SMALL SHALLOT, SLICED PAPER THIN

1 TBSP FRESH LEMON JUICE

¼ TSP SUGAR

1 TSP OLIVE OIL

4 CELERY STALKS

KOSHER SALT AND FRESHLY GROUND BLACK PEPPER

Makes 1 cup [150 g] Put the sliced shallot in a small bowl of ice water to soak until you're ready to use it.

In a medium bowl, whisk together the lemon juice, sugar, and olive oil.

Shave the celery on a mandoline, or thinly slice with a sharp knife, reserving any intact verdant leaves. Remove the shallots from the water and pat dry with a paper towel. Add the celery, celery leaves, and shallot to the dressing and toss. Season with salt and pepper.

Perfectly Dressed Herb Salad

This miniature salad might look like something designed for a woodland creature, but a pile of perfectly dressed herbs can turn a pretty good tinned fish spread into one you might pay money for at a fancy restaurant. (The herb salad is one reason I love ordering from the tin menu at Essex Pearl, in New York's Essex Market.) A gentle toss with olive oil and champagne vinegar brings out the natural crunch and freshness in herbs like parsley and chives, and it keeps them from tasting too dry when piled onto a sandwich, like the Triple Pickle Smoked Salmon Butter Sandwich (page 150). You can keep it simple when you're making this mix for a sandwich or for your own weeknight sardine-and-bread dinner. But if you're incorporating this into a party spread, you can toss in some chive blossoms, calendula petals, or whatever pretty, edible things you have growing in your yard.

1 CUP [12 G] FRESH FLAT-LEAF PARSLEY LEAVES

¼ CUP [3 G] TORN FRESH DILL (SMALL PIECES)

¼ CUP [3 G] CUT-UP FRESH CHIVES (½ IN [13 MM] LENGTHS)

½ TSP CHAMPAGNE VINEGAR

½ TSP OLIVE OIL

PINCH OF FLAKY SEA SALT

3 GRINDS OF BLACK PEPPER

Makes 1½ cups [20 g]   Toss together the parsley leaves, dill, and chives in a small bowl. In a small measuring cup or jar, whisk together the vinegar and olive oil. Gently pour the dressing down the sides of the bowl, and use two forks to carefully toss the herbs without bruising or crushing them. Once the greens are evenly coated, sprinkle with the salt and pepper, and give one last toss. Use immediately.

Crispy Fried Capers

I'll always happily spoon capers onto a bagel covered with smoked salmon, or into a butter sauce for poaching a halibut fillet. But when these briny little flavor bombs are fried, they're transformed into something sultry and sophisticated. The hot oil strips away the clammy chill of the refrigerator, and pulls the petals away from the buds, so you're left with what looks like a pile of tiny, crunchy flowers. With their pickled flavor, they're perfect for sprinkling over a great smoked trout or toast piled high with oil-packed mackerel.

2 TBSP CAPERS PACKED IN BRINE

3 TBSP OLIVE OIL

Makes 2 Tbsp Spread out the capers on a paper towel to absorb any moisture.

In a small skillet, heat the olive oil over medium heat for about 2 minutes. The oil is hot enough when a caper added to the skillet bubbles and sizzles. Add the capers and give them a quick stir to distribute. The pan will sputter, so stand back. Fry the capers for 3 minutes, or until the bubbling has died down and the capers are golden brown, stirring a couple times while they cook.

With a slotted spoon, remove the capers and drain on a paper towel. Save the cooking oil for salad dressing or for cooking your next frittata.

Green Anchovy Butter

Packing a massive amount of umami, anchovies have some pretty big star power straight out of the can. But when they're suspended in butter—all the better with a smattering of fresh herbs and garlic—the sky's the limit. Use this butter to baste a seared steak as it finishes cooking in the skillet. Melt the butter and pour it over popcorn, or cook an egg in it. You can add equal parts flour and transform the flavor bomb into savory shortbreads, like those on page 99. Or you can slather it onto some great bread with some juicy slices of tomato like the toasts on page 77.

½ CUP [113 G] UNSALTED BUTTER, AT ROOM TEMPERATURE

5 ANCHOVY FILLETS IN OLIVE OIL

½ CUP [6 G] FRESH FLAT-LEAF PARSLEY LEAVES

1 TSP FRESH LEMON JUICE

½ TSP GRATED LEMON ZEST

1 GARLIC CLOVE

5 GRINDS OF BLACK PEPPER

Makes ½ cup [113 g] In a blender (or in a 1 pt [475 ml] jar with an immersion blender), combine all the ingredients and whir until the parsley and anchovies appear to be evenly distributed throughout the butter. Taste, and season with more pepper as needed (the anchovies should have you well covered on the salt front). Store in a tightly sealed container for up to 5 days.

EVERY LAST ANCHOVY

Sometimes I get a little teary-eyed when I think of all of the tins of anchovies that have been opened for the sake of adding a couple fillets to a recipe, only to be thrown out three months later, when they're discovered rotting away in the back of the refrigerator. I, too, have made this mistake, sighing as I throw away the remains of a good six-dollar can. So much potential for umami, squandered!

Many home cooks don't realize this, but unlike many other tinned seafoods, anchovies are only partially preserved. This means that even in an unopened can, they shouldn't be stored for much more than a year, after which they start to become mushy, grainy, and unpleasant in taste. I store my unopened tins in the refrigerator to slow this process. A few European brands explicitly remind you on the package to store them in the refrigerator.

Once a tin of anchovies is opened, the fillets start to break down even more quickly. With some conscientious storage and clever improvisation as you cook over the course of a month, these tiny fish can avoid the fate of so many before them.

STORE WISELY

Exposure to air can speed the oxidation process that breaks down anchovies, so rather than haphazardly covering the open tin with cling wrap or foil, transfer the remaining fish to a small, resealable, airtight container, like a spice jar. Pour a little extra olive oil into the jar so the fish are completely submerged. Store in the refrigerator and try to use up within a week.

BRAISE AWAY

Anchovies dissolve easily into big, simmering pots of sauces and stews, adding a subtle savory layer that's hard to match. I love to add a couple of fillets to a big pot of white beans, a spicy tomato sauce, or a slow-cooked pork shoulder in the last hour of cooking.

BUTTER UP

Folding minced anchovies into butter can do wonders for so many foods, like a steak seared in a cast-iron skillet. Try rubbing the Green Anchovy Butter (page 59) over the skin of a chicken before roasting. Or mash some anchovies and add them to garlic butter for your popcorn. (See the Caesar Popcorn on page 92.)

TOAST TIME

For a million-dollar snack in mere minutes, put some olive oil–brushed toast on a grill or under a broiler until it's slightly charred, rub the surface with a raw garlic clove, and spread a few anchovy fillets across it. If you like, top with a few slices of tomato or avocado or a scoop of ricotta.

MAKE IT A DRESSING

A Caesar dressing (page 65), is an obvious option for leftover anchovy fillets, but consider mincing a few anchovies and whisking them into simpler vinaigrettes, too, with some minced shallot, olive oil, and white wine vinegar.

Romesco Sauce

Romesco is a nutty, salty, and slightly sweet pepper sauce often paired with fish in Spanish cooking. Though there are infinite variations involving hazelnuts, walnuts, fresh peppers, and dried chiles, I usually opt for roasted red peppers straight from the jar, a handful of almonds, and a heel of bread (which makes the sauce silkier), all juiced up with plenty of olive oil, sherry vinegar, and garlic. It adds a flash of fiery orange color to a plate, but it can also bring a fruity, smoky dose of acidity to tinned fish. Try this on a toast, like the Romesco Mackerel Toast with Fried Capers (page 78), or alongside a snack spread of tinned mussels, sardines, and crunchy vegetables.

½ CUP [110 G] PACKED ROASTED RED PEPPERS FROM A JAR

¼ CUP [35 G] ROASTED SALTED ALMONDS

1 GARLIC CLOVE

¼ CUP [60 ML] OLIVE OIL, PLUS 1 TBSP IF NEEDED

2 TBSP SHERRY VINEGAR

ONE 1 IN [2.5 CM] LONG HEEL OF A BAGUETTE

PINCH OF KOSHER SALT

PINCH OF FRESHLY GROUND BLACK PEPPER

PINCH OF SMOKED PAPRIKA

Makes ¾ cup [180 ml]   Combine all the ingredients in a blender or food processor, and blend for about 1 minute, until smooth and creamy. If the consistency is pasty, add 1 more tablespoon of olive oil. Serve immediately, or store in a tightly covered container in the refrigerator for up to 3 days.

Tonnato Sauce

Tonnato is a cool, creamy, wonderfully fishy sauce that traditionally adorns thin slices of simmered veal in Piedmontese cuisine. Tuna, anchovies, capers, and mayo come together in a rich, silky emulsified sauce that's sort of like a more robust Caesar dressing. It makes a great base for other salads, too, like Grilled Radicchio with Fresh Tomatoes & Tonnato (page 129). And it's thick enough to slather onto a sandwich filled with grilled vegetables. For quickly made deviled eggs, dollop tonnato onto halved Beet-Pickled Eggs (page 120) and sprinkle with capers.

ONE 5 TO 6 OZ [140 TO 170 G] CAN TUNA IN OLIVE OIL, UNDRAINED

½ CUP [105 G] MAYONNAISE

2 TBSP CAPERS

¼ CUP [60 ML] FRESH LEMON JUICE

4 ANCHOVY FILLETS IN OLIVE OIL

Makes 1½ cups [360 ml] In a blender (or a large jar, if you're using an immersion blender), combine all the ingredients. Blend for about 1 minute, or until the entire mixture takes on a smooth, creamy, and uniform texture. Scrape down the sides, and blend for 15 seconds more. Transfer to a glass jar or plastic container, cover tightly, and refrigerate until you're ready to use. It will keep for up to 3 days.

My Go-To Vinaigrette

This is my take on a classic French vinaigrette, which comes in handy whether I'm turning a little pile of greens into a side salad for the Smoked Salmon, Caramelized Onion & Fresh Pea Frittata (page 184), or just marinating some blanched asparagus to eat with a poached egg. It's also the key to the Everything Pink Salad (page 143) and the Late-Summer Niçoise with Fresh Corn & Cherry Tomatoes (page 139). Letting a smashed clove of garlic infuse the vinaigrette gives it some bite, and a tiny bit of sugar softens the acidity. I opt for a not-too-salty vinaigrette, because I love to shower my finished salads with some crunchy, flaky sea salt (not to mention the occasional anchovy fillet or mountain of grated Parmesan). But season the vinaigrette to your own taste.

½ CUP [120 ML] OLIVE OIL

½ CUP [120 ML] RED WINE VINEGAR

1 GARLIC CLOVE, LIGHTLY SMASHED

2 TSP SUGAR

2 TSP DIJON MUSTARD (I LIKE MAILLE)

⅛ TSP SALT

⅛ TSP FRESHLY GROUND BLACK PEPPER

Makes 1 cup [240 ml]   In a small glass jar, combine all the ingredients and shake vigorously. Let sit for at least 30 minutes to allow the garlic to infuse the other ingredients and to let the sugar and salt dissolve. Shake again vigorously before using to emulsify. The vinaigrette will keep, tightly covered in the refrigerator, for up to 1 week.

Lemony Caesar Dressing

Caesar dressing might be the best thing that's ever happened to the anchovy. This luxurious dressing opened the floodgate to anchovy fandom for hundreds of thousands (probably even millions) of people through the years. I double down on the anchovy flavor by adding a touch of Worcestershire sauce. And I add plenty of black pepper, because the creaminess of the emulsified egg yolk and oil holds up to a lot of bite. This dressing is a great match for a classic Caesar, like the Little Gems Caesar with Challah Bread Crumbs & Black Sesame (page 125), but also try drizzling it over some grilled green beans or roasted broccoli.

1 EGG YOLK

3 ANCHOVY FILLETS IN OLIVE OIL, MINCED

1 SMALL GARLIC CLOVE, MINCED

2 TBSP CANOLA OIL

2 TBSP OLIVE OIL

¼ CUP [8 G] GRATED PARMESAN CHEESE

2 TBSP FRESH LEMON JUICE

¼ TSP WORCESTERSHIRE SAUCE

15 GRINDS OF BLACK PEPPER

Makes ½ cup [120 ml]   In a small jar, combine the egg yolk, anchovies, and garlic. With an immersion blender, pulse until well combined. With the immersion blender running, add the canola oil in a slow, steady stream. The mixture should start to take on the appearance of heavy cream. With the blender still running, add the olive oil in a slow, steady stream. Add the Parmesan, lemon juice, Worcestershire sauce, and black pepper, and blend until the mixture is emulsified into a thick dressing. (Alternatively, in a small bowl, whisk together vigorously the egg yolk, anchovies, and garlic. Add the oils slowly, while whisking, and then the remaining ingredients.)

Use immediately, or cover the jar tightly and store in the refrigerator for up to 3 days.

SNACK TIME

When it's almost time for lunch or dinner, and I have no battle plan in place and no time for a grocery run, one of my most oft-repeated templates is what I call the snack meal. It's a true win for any discerning, but slightly lazy, home cook because it's an excuse to use up whatever odds and ends you have sitting around your kitchen, along with some tinned fish. And it makes you feel like you're at a party, taking itinerant jumps from bite to bite.

Toast up some bread from the night before, slather it with Green Anchovy Butter (page 59), and stack it with juicy slices of tomato. Or steam some rice and toss it quickly with oily mackerel and plenty of nori and sesame seed–flecked furikake for a batch of fresh, warm onigiri. For an easy snack, toss a tin of amazing mussels in escabeche sauce over a bowl of potato chips, and add a few green olives and a dash of hot sauce. Mix and match a few of these, and then it's *really* a party.

The recipes in this chapter will bring some fun to any occasion, whether it's a harried weekday lunch, an after-work meetup with friends at the park, or to accompany a bottle of wine when unexpected guests drop in.

Smoked Trout Dip

Topped with neon orange trout roe and a confetti of chives, this salty, smoky dip makes an eye-catching centerpiece when served with a platter of crudités or a big pile of sturdy potato chips. Most people I know would also happily eat it heaped onto a bagel, with a slice of tomato and a sliver of red onion.

I love to make this with JOSE Gourmet's smoked trout, which comes in rectangular tins containing two tidy fillets with their sequined silver skin still intact. Packed in olive oil, the fish has a tender, delicate texture that gives it a remarkably fresh taste. A great alternative that's less expensive and easier to find is Trader Joe's smoked trout in a can, a handy ingredient to have around for adding a bit of protein to salads or breakfast scrambles.

ONE 3½ TO 4 OZ [100 TO 115 G] CAN SMOKED TROUT IN OLIVE OIL OR CANOLA OIL (SUCH AS JOSE GOURMET OR TRADER JOE'S), DRAINED

½ CUP (4 OZ [115 G]) CREAM CHEESE, AT ROOM TEMPERATURE

½ CUP (4 OZ [115 G]) CRÈME FRAÎCHE

2 TSP MINCED SHALLOT

1 TSP FRESH LEMON JUICE, PLUS MORE AS NEEDED

PINCH OF FRESHLY GROUND BLACK PEPPER

MINCED FRESH CHIVES, FOR GARNISH (OPTIONAL)

TROUT ROE, FOR GARNISH (OPTIONAL)

Makes 1¼ cups [330 g] In a small bowl, use a fork to mix together the trout, cream cheese, crème fraîche, shallot, lemon juice, and pepper, flaking the fish apart as you mix.

Taste the dip and add more lemon juice or pepper, if needed (it should already be quite salty from the fish). Transfer the dip to a small serving bowl, and top with the minced chives and trout roe, if using. Store any dip you're not eating immediately in a tightly covered container in the refrigerator for up to 3 days.

Whipped Potato Cod Dip

Salted and dried cod is the basis for a classic French dip called brandade. For brandade, you generally soak the cod to rehydrate it and eliminate some of the salt, and then simmer it in milk. The tender fish is then mixed with boiled potatoes and cream, and baked in a casserole dish until it's warm and golden brown on top. Using tinned cod packed in olive oil—like the ones Bela, JOSE Gourmet, and Briosa Gourmet make—cuts down on the long, arduous rehydration process, and it also has a sweeter flavor and more tender texture. This version can be served warm, cold, or at room temperature in an earthenware crock with a few slices of chewy sourdough.

1 WHITE POTATO (4 OZ [115 G]), PEELED AND HALVED

3 GARLIC CLOVES

1 TSP KOSHER SALT

ONE 4 OZ [115 G] TIN COD IN OLIVE OIL, UNDRAINED

3 TBSP CRÈME FRAÎCHE

FRESHLY GROUND BLACK PEPPER

1 TBSP MINCED FRESH CHIVES

Makes 1½ cups [400 g] In a small saucepan, combine the potato, garlic, and salt, and add enough water to cover the potatoes. Place over medium heat, bring to a boil, lower the heat, and simmer for about 20 minutes, or until the potato falls apart easily when poked with a fork.

With a slotted spoon, transfer the potato and garlic to a medium bowl, setting aside the salty, garlicky cooking water. Remove the cod from its tin, reserving the oil, and add to the bowl. With a hand mixer on high speed, beat the mixture together, gradually adding 1 or 2 Tbsp of the cooking water at a time, until the mixture has the texture of a smooth dip. You will need about 4 Tbsp [60 ml] of the cooking water in total. Add the crème fraîche and a few grinds of black pepper and beat until incorporated. Spoon the dip into a crock or shallow serving bowl. Drizzle with the oil from the tin, sprinkle with more black pepper, and garnish with the chives.

Baked Clam Dip
with Bacon & Green Onions

Clam dip means different things to different people. The dip can be cool and creamy and lemony, or packed full of melted cheese and warm garlic. In this slightly retro version, bacon, green onions, and cream cheese come together in a smoky, salty combination that just might become your new favorite snack to bring, oven ready, to potlucks with a sleeve of Ritz crackers or baguette rounds for dipping. The dip will taste even better if it has time for the flavors to meld, so consider making this the night before and baking it the next day.

4 SLICES BACON

3 GREEN ONIONS (WHITE AND GREEN PARTS), MINCED

ONE 8 OZ [230 G] BRICK CREAM CHEESE, AT ROOM TEMPERATURE

TWO 6½ OZ [185 G] CANS CHOPPED OR MINCED CLAMS, DRAINED

¼ TSP HOT SAUCE

¼ TSP WORCESTERSHIRE SAUCE

½ TSP FRESH LEMON JUICE

SLICED BAGUETTE, WAVY POTATO CHIPS, OR BUTTERY CRACKERS, FOR SERVING

Serves 6 to 8   Preheat the oven to 350°F [180°C].

In a large, heavy-bottomed skillet over medium heat, cook the bacon until dark brown and crisp, about 3 minutes per side. Transfer to a paper towel–lined plate and let cool. Finely chop into crumbles.

Set aside about a third of the bacon and a third of the green onion. Put the remaining bacon and green onion in a medium bowl and add the cream cheese, clams, hot sauce, Worcestershire sauce, and lemon juice.

Transfer the mixture to a 10 to 12 oz [300 to 360 ml] ramekin or gratin dish (a mini–loaf pan will work in a pinch). Garnish with the reserved bacon. (If making ahead, cover the ramekin with aluminum foil and refrigerate.) Bake for 30 minutes, or until the top begins to brown. Top with the reserved green onions, and serve hot with the baguette slices, potato chips, or crackers.

Tomato Tartine

with Green Anchovy Butter

Whenever I wind up with part of a loaf of good sourdough left over from dinner, I like to slice it, put it in a ziplock bag, and keep it in the freezer for toast. This comes in extremely handy during tomato season, when the heirlooms sitting on the countertop have just a few fleeting days of perfect ripeness, and they beg to be sliced and turned into an open-faced tartine. And it's made all the better when you have a salty, herby, garlic-packed anchovy butter in the refrigerator. This makes a breezy lunch for two, or you could cut each toast in half and fill a tray with them for a predinner party bite.

4 SLICES GOOD SOURDOUGH BREAD

1 LARGE (ABOUT 14 OZ [400 G]) RIPE HEIRLOOM TOMATO

4 TBSP [55 G] GREEN ANCHOVY BUTTER (PAGE 59), AT ROOM TEMPERATURE

FLAKY SEA SALT AND FRESHLY GROUND BLACK PEPPER

Makes 4 toasts   Toast the bread until it's warmed through and just slightly crisp on the surface, but not brittle. Or place the slices on a baking sheet under the broiler for about 1 minute, rearranging the slices if they start to brown.

Let the toast cool slightly while you slice your tomato into thin, even slices, about ¼ in [6 mm] thick. Spread 1 Tbsp of the butter onto each slice of bread, and top with tomato slices. Sprinkle with salt and pepper.

Romesco Mackerel Toast

with Fried Capers

Mackerel has a wonderfully mild flavor, much like tuna, but the meat is more delicate. I love the way it tastes with a romesco sauce full of roasted almonds, roasted red peppers, and smoked paprika. This warm, smoky toast would make a happy addition to a pot of soup for a dinner party, or you could serve it alongside a salad and a charcuterie spread. Rubbing the warm bread with garlic gives it a little bite without distracting from the fruity, smoky romesco or the tender flakes of fish.

½ BAGUETTE (ABOUT 8 OZ [225 G])

1 TBSP OLIVE OIL

1 GARLIC CLOVE

1 RECIPE ROMESCO SAUCE (PAGE 62)

ONE 3 TO 4 OZ [85 TO 115 G] TIN MACKEREL FILLETS IN OLIVE OIL (SUCH AS MATIZ, MINERVA, PATAGONIA, OR JOSE GOURMET), DRAINED

1 RECIPE CRISPY FRIED CAPERS (PAGE 58)

½ CUP [5 G] FRESH FLAT-LEAF PARSLEY LEAVES

Makes 6 toasts   Preheat the broiler. Cut the baguette in half lengthwise, and then cut each half into three slices. Arrange the slices on a baking sheet and brush the cut surface of the bread with the olive oil. Broil for about 2 minutes, or until parts of the bread are just beginning to toast and char slightly.

Rub the garlic clove across the surface of each slice. Divide the romesco sauce among the toasts, spreading it lightly. Flake apart the mackerel fillets into bite-size pieces, and sprinkle across the surface of each toast. Sprinkle the toasts with the capers and parsley leaves. Eat immediately.

Sardine Curry Puffs

Curry puffs, or epok epok, are a popular Singaporean street snack that can be filled with ground beef, durian, chicken, or canned sardines, and are fragrant with ginger, garlic, and fresh curry leaves. I first got to know these savory pastries when the journalist and filmmaker Natalie Pattillo wrote for *TASTE* about her mother's beef curry puff recipe—a recipe that's made waves at several generations of birthday parties, graduations, weddings, and baby showers in Natalie's family. This is her sardine spin on the recipe. Sardines in tomato sauce are enlivened with fresh aromatics, warm spices, and lime juice, and then wrapped in buttery dough and fried into the perfect handheld snack. Show up to a party with these, and you will leave with a lot of new friends.

FILLING

2 TBSP CANOLA OIL

2 SMALL SHALLOTS, DICED

1 SPRIG FRESH CURRY LEAVES, FINELY CHOPPED

ONE 1 IN [2.5 CM] PIECE GINGER, PEELED AND GRATED

4 GARLIC CLOVES, MINCED

1 JALAPEÑO PEPPER, DICED

1 TBSP CURRY POWDER

½ TSP GROUND CUMIN

1 SMALL RUSSET POTATO (3½ OZ [100 G]), FINELY DICED

TWO 4 OZ [115 G] CANS SARDINES IN TOMATO SAUCE (SUCH AS BELA OR WILD PLANET), UNDRAINED

JUICE OF 1 LIME, OR 2 CALAMANSI

KOSHER SALT AND WHITE PEPPER

con't

Makes 16 to 18 puffs   TO MAKE THE FILLING: In a large skillet, heat the canola oil over medium heat. Add the shallots, curry leaves, ginger, garlic, and jalapeño, and sauté until lightly browned, about 5 minutes. Add the curry powder and cumin, and sauté for 2 minutes more.

Add the potato cubes and stir to coat them with the spices. Cook until the potato softens, about 5 to 7 minutes, and then add the sardines and the tomato sauce from the cans. Break up the sardines and stir to combine. Add the lime juice and season with the salt and white pepper. Cook for about 2 minutes more and remove from the heat. Let cool while you prepare the dough.

con't

DOUGH

¾ TSP KOSHER SALT

3 CUPS [420 G] ALL-PURPOSE FLOUR, PLUS 3 OR 4 TBSP MORE, AS NEEDED

1 CUP [226 G] GHEE OR MARGARINE, MELTED

CANOLA OIL, FOR FRYING THE PUFFS

TO MAKE THE DOUGH: Stir the salt into 1 cup [240 ml] of cold water until it dissolves. Put the flour in a large bowl, and gradually add the salt water, mixing it into the flour with your hands. Mix in the melted ghee with your hands. If the dough feels too wet, add a little more flour.

Knead the dough in the bowl or on a clean, lightly floured surface until smooth. Divide into sixteen to eighteen equal balls the size of golf balls and place on a baking sheet. Cover with plastic wrap and allow the dough to rest for 15 minutes.

On a clean, lightly floured surface, flatten each dough ball with a rolling pin until it's about 4 to 5 in [10 to 13 cm] in diameter. Place 1½ to 2 Tbsp of filling into the center of each. Fold the dough over the filling into a semicircle and gently press closed. Twist the seam into a spiraling rope pattern by pinching and folding along the entire edge (there are some handy YouTube tutorials about how to get this movement just right), then press with a fork to seal.

Heat about 1 in [2.5 cm] of canola oil in a large, heavy-bottomed Dutch oven over medium heat. Line a baking sheet with paper towels. When the oil is hot and a tiny pinch of flour bubbles in it, gently lower a batch (about four) of the curry puffs into the oil and cook for 2 to 3 minutes, or until the bottoms are golden brown. Turn over and fry for 2 to 3 minutes more. Use a slotted spoon to remove from the pan and drain on the prepared baking sheet. Repeat with the remaining curry puffs and eat within 2 hours for maximum crispiness.

Canned Clam Garlic Bread

When Tony Liu decided to put a clam garlic bread on the menu of his Jackson Heights restaurant, the Queensboro, it was a nod to the linguine with clam sauce that his dad used to make for him when he was growing up in Hawaii. Tony's technique of reducing the brine to a flavorful sauce to mix with butter is ingenious enough to spin a few cheap cans into dinner gold. The garlic cooks in the oven, the bread gets perfectly crusty, and the clams come out juicy and tender—just like they would on a perfectly cooked clam pie.

My adaptation of Tony's recipe doubles down on the clams, making the bread hearty enough to make a meal of it, especially when served with a big, delicious salad. If you don't think you'll eat the whole baguette in one sitting, cut the buttered loaf into segments before baking. Wrap each segment you want to save in aluminum foil, place in a freezer bag, and store in your freezer to eat with future bowls of fagioli or squares of lasagna. When you unwrap the frozen garlic bread, bake it as instructed, adding an extra 7 to 10 minutes of baking time.

TWO 6½ OZ [185 G] CANS CHOPPED CLAMS IN BRINE (SUCH AS BAR HARBOR FOODS), UNDRAINED

½ CUP [113 G] UNSALTED BUTTER, CUT INTO 3 OR 4 PIECES

¼ CUP [8 G] GRATED PARMESAN CHEESE

GRATED ZEST OF 1 LEMON

5 GARLIC CLOVES, MINCED

¼ CUP [8 G] MINCED FRESH FLAT-LEAF PARSLEY

⅛ TSP RED PEPPER FLAKES, PLUS MORE AS NEEDED

1 BAGUETTE

KOSHER SALT (OPTIONAL)

Serves 4 to 6   Preheat the oven to 300°F [150°C].

Drain all of the brine from the tins of clams into a medium saucepan. Bring to a simmer over medium heat and continue simmering for about 15 minutes, until reduced to about ¼ cup [60 ml]. Remove from the heat and stir in the butter until melted.

con't

While the butter and brine mixture cools slightly, in a small bowl, mix together the chopped clams, Parmesan, lemon zest, garlic, parsley, and red pepper flakes.

Cut the baguette in half lengthwise, but not all the way through, so that you can open it up without breaking the two halves apart. Place, cut-side up, on a baking sheet.

Add the chopped clam mixture to the butter and brine mixture and toss thoroughly. Taste and add more red pepper flakes if needed. The reduced clam juice should provide all the salt you want but add a pinch more if needed.

Spoon the clam butter mixture over the cut surface of the bread, spreading it all the way to the edges. Bake for 20 for 25 minutes, or until the surface is golden brown and the bread is crusty and crunchy on the outside.

WAIT, DON'T THROW OUT THE BRINE!

When you finish a tin of really good razor clams or cockles, or when you've just tossed a tin's worth of chopped clams into a skillet for some linguine, the temptation is always there: It would be *so* easy to just tip the remaining pale, milky liquid right down the drain.

Resist the urge! Some people would pay good money for that brine. Brands like Bar Harbor, Snow's, and Cento even bottle and sell the salty juice from clams to add to brothy seafood dishes. And often, the really high-quality shellfish are packed in a brine with its own character, nuances, and subtle sweetness. But even the liquid left over from an inexpensive can of clams from the supermarket is packed with umami, which can come in extremely handy when you cook. Think of it as the ocean's own MSG.

Next time you find yourself with some extra brine, transfer it to a small jar and refrigerate it for a few days, or pour it into a plastic container and freeze it for up to 3 months. With these tips in your back pocket, you'll make the most of it.

DRINK IT

Okay, maybe not on its own. But consider adding a splash of brine to your next martini in place of the olive brine for a clean, mineral salinity. You can also use this brine to turn your next Bloody Mary into a delicious Bloody Caesar with freshly made tomato juice, lemon juice, some grated horseradish, and vodka.

SIMMER SMARTLY

If you're planning to simmer a fillet of cod or halibut in a spicy tomato sauce later in the week, set aside some clam brine to add to the sauce. It will provide a savory flavor base that a lot of mild white fish don't have on their own. You can also add a splash to a pot of mussels simmering in white wine. You won't notice the clam flavor, but the brine will bring out all the mussels' best qualities.

MAKE A POT OF RICE

Planning your next shrimp risotto or seafood paella? A splash of reserved clam brine will bring a more concentrated ocean flavor than most seafood stocks, and the little bit of added salt will help flavor each grain of rice from the inside out.

WHEN IN DOUBT, REDUCE, REUSE, RECYCLE

If you don't have anything brothy or vodka-fueled in your eating and drinking plans for the near future, you can always reduce the brine by half over low heat to create a potent elixir, which you can whirl into a compound butter or turn into a quick sauce with some garlic, white wine, and olive oil. This trick is used in both the Canned Clam Garlic Bread (page 83) and the Spaghetti with Fancy Clams & Fancy Ham (page 178).

Spicy Tuna Kimbap

The first time I had Eunjo Park's famous kimbap, it was at Momofuku Kāwi, where she was chef from 2019 to 2021, when the restaurant closed. The crackly toasted seaweed wrapping gave way to tender, sesame-scented rice, which in turn was wrapped around creamy foie gras, crunchy daikon, and fresh chives. It was a perfect bite. But of course, kimbap, one of Korea's most famous dishes, doesn't need foie gras to be a perfect bite. Often brought along to picnics and packed in lunches, the rolls can be stuffed with steamed vegetables, pickles, thin ribbons of omelet, and, of course, tinned fish.

Eunjo shared with me her favorite way to turn canned tuna into a filling—by mixing it with spicy, umami-packed gochujang and mayo, and wrapping it in perilla leaves before tucking it into the center of each roll. The perilla leaves (a member of the mint family) add a lovely cooling effect, which balances the heat. It's all complemented by danmuji (sweet-ened pickled daikon) and plenty of crunchy vegetables. While this recipe requires some initial prep to cut, mix, season, and cook some of the fill-ings, the assembly itself is remarkably quick and easy, and the payoff is possibly the most exciting lunch you'll ever pack for yourself. If you can't find perilla, the kimbap will still taste great, but definitely seek it out if you have a Korean grocery store nearby.

con't

1⅓ CUPS [265 G] SHORT-GRAIN WHITE RICE

1 TBSP PLUS 1 TSP TOASTED SESAME OIL

1 TBSP TOASTED SESAME SEEDS

KOSHER SALT

1 BUNCH SPINACH (9 OZ [255 G]), CAREFULLY WASHED

3 EGGS

1 TBSP CANOLA OIL

1 MEDIUM CARROT, PEELED AND JULIENNED

TWO 5 OZ [140 G] CANS TUNA IN WATER (SUCH AS DONGWON), DRAINED

½ CUP [105 G] MAYONNAISE

3 TBSP GOCHUJANG

8 SHEETS ROASTED SEAWEED

10 FRESH PERILLA LEAVES

1 SMALL CUCUMBER, OR 2 PERSIAN CUCUMBERS, JULIENNED

ONE 3 IN [7.5 CM] LENGTH DANMUJI, CUT INTO THICK MATCHSTICKS

Serves 4 to 6   Rinse the rice under cold running water until the water runs clear. Drain thoroughly and cook it in a rice cooker or on the stove top according to the instructions on the package. With the rice cooker paddle or a wooden spatula, gently fold in 1 Tbsp of the sesame oil, the sesame seeds, and ½ tsp salt.

Fill a medium saucepan with water and bring to a boil. Meanwhile, fill a medium bowl with ice water to keep nearby. Once the water in the pan is boiling, lower the spinach into it for 30 seconds. It's important to work quickly here, so that the spinach doesn't lose all of its freshness or crunch. Use a slotted spoon to quickly transfer the blanched spinach to the prepared ice bath. Let cool completely, and drain, gently squeezing out any additional water. Transfer to a small bowl. Loosen the spinach gently with a fork and toss it with ½ tsp of sesame oil and a pinch of salt.

In a small bowl, whisk together the eggs with a pinch of salt. In a small nonstick skillet, heat the canola oil over medium-low heat. Add the carrot and cook, stirring frequently, for about 3 minutes, or just until the carrots have softened slightly. Transfer them to a plate or bowl, leaving the remaining oil in the pan. Sprinkle the carrots with a pinch of salt.

Pour the eggs into the skillet and tilt the pan from side to side to distribute them to the edges, like a crêpe. After about 2 minutes, when the eggs are starting to set in one large pancake, use a wide plastic spatula to flip the pancake, and cook for about 1 minute longer, until just set. Remove the egg round to a cutting board, and cut into long, very thin strips.

In a medium bowl, thoroughly mix the tuna with the mayonnaise and gochujang.

Place a dry cutting board in front of you to use as a work surface for rolling the kimbap. Place the other ingredients nearby, so that they're handy as you work. Set down a sheet of seaweed and cover three-quarters of the surface with a thin layer of rice, starting with the edge closest to you (leaving a border of seaweed will help seal up the roll). Cut three sheets of seaweed in half, and center one half sheet on top of the rice layer (this will help insulate the wet vegetables so that the rice doesn't get soggy).

Now, set two of the perilla leaves down on top of the smaller piece of seaweed, and top with a line of the tuna mixture that extends from one end of the roll to the other. Roll the perilla around the tuna to make a cigar shape. Add a small handful each of the spinach, carrot, egg, cucumber, and danmuji, extending across the length of the seaweed.

Gently but firmly roll the entire rectangle into a tight log, and place seam-side down on a plate. Repeat for a total of five rolls. Brush the tops of the rolls with the remaining ½ tsp of sesame oil and cut each log into eight to twelve slices. Serve immediately.

Caesar Popcorn

This popcorn, thrown together from a smattering of pantry ingredients, manages to channel some of the best attributes of garlic knots (the warm garlic butter and chopped parsley) with the richness of a Caesar salad (the lemon, anchovy, and healthy dose of black pepper). And yet, you can make it in fewer than 10 minutes. Add an extra 5 minutes, and you can even get a batch of icy Negronis together to sip between salty bites. To keep the popcorn from getting soggy, make sure you dry the parsley thoroughly before chopping and eat the popcorn while it's warm.

2 TBSP CANOLA OIL

¼ CUP [50 G] UNPOPPED, UNFLAVORED POPCORN KERNELS

3 ANCHOVY FILLETS IN OLIVE OIL, DRAINED

1 SMALL GARLIC CLOVE, GRATED

1½ TBSP BUTTER

1 TSP FINELY CHOPPED FRESH FLAT-LEAF PARSLEY

1 TBSP FINELY GRATED PARMESAN CHEESE

¼ TSP GRATED LEMON ZEST

FRESHLY GROUND BLACK PEPPER

Serves 4   In a medium Dutch oven or metal pot with a lid, heat the canola oil over medium heat for about 1 minute. Add the popcorn kernels and cover. As the kernels begin to pop, gently tilt the pot from side to side to distribute the kernels across the bottom, while keeping the lid firmly closed to avoid any of the hot steam escaping. When the popping has slowed down, and there are several seconds of silence between pops, remove the pot from the heat. Keep the lid on.

Mince the anchovies and use the side of a knife to mash them into a paste. Transfer to a small microwave-safe bowl and add the garlic and butter. Microwave for several seconds, watching carefully, until the butter has melted.

Transfer the popcorn to a serving bowl and toss with the warm anchovy and garlic butter. Sprinkle with the parsley, Parmesan, lemon zest, and black pepper, and serve immediately.

Bagna Cauda
with French Breakfast Radishes

Bagna cauda is one of my favorite ways to showcase great anchovies. At its simplest, the dip consists of just gently warmed butter, olive oil, minced anchovies, and garlic. I like to use an immersion blender at the end, because it both emulsifies the dressing and collects the anchovy bones in its blades. The result is a pleasantly smooth dip with a punch in every bite.

The warm dip is often served with crisp vegetables as a snack, sometimes sitting over a small burner to keep it warm and fill the air with the smell of garlic. The vegetables can include endives, Romanesco broccoli, carrots, or fennel, but to me, there's nothing quite like the juxtaposition of a crisp, spicy radish and a warm, sultry bagna cauda, especially when that radish has been spritzed lightly with lemon juice. If you have leftover bagna cauda, try tossing roasted broccoli and chickpeas in it and finishing the dish with lots of lemon juice and fresh mint.

¼ CUP [60 ML] OLIVE OIL

6 GARLIC CLOVES, MINCED

8 ANCHOVY FILLETS IN OLIVE OIL, DRAINED

4 TBSP [55 G] BUTTER

1 BUNCH [250 G] BREAKFAST RADISHES OR ASSORTED RADISHES, STEMS TRIMMED AND RADISHES HALVED

½ TSP FRESH LEMON JUICE

Serves 4   In a small saucepan, heat the olive oil over low heat. Add the garlic and anchovies, and cook, stirring gently, for about 5 minutes, or until the anchovies have broken down and dissolved into the oil, and the garlic smells potent.

Stir in the butter until melted and remove from the heat. Using an immersion blender, blend in the saucepan for 2 or 3 minutes, or until the mixture has emulsified into a thick dressing. Transfer to a small serving bowl.

In another small serving bowl, toss the radishes with the lemon juice. Serve them alongside the warm bagna cauda.

Gildas

Gildas are a quintessential Basque pintxo, a salty, dainty drinking snack. These little skewers combine anchovies, olives, and pickled peppers into a single explosively briny bite, which will be very welcome between sips of an afternoon beer or vermouth.

In Spain, boquerónes, lightly salted anchovies marinated in vinegar, are often used for gildas, but I love the deep umami quality of canned anchovies in olive oil, especially when paired with the acidity and spice of piparra peppers (pickled guindilla peppers). Since you'll be artfully skewering the anchovy fillets, buy a good-quality can, so the anchovies won't fall apart in your hands.

10 PIPARRA PEPPERS

10 PITTED CASTELVETRANO OLIVES

10 INTACT ANCHOVIES IN OLIVE OIL (SUCH AS ORTIZ OR DON BOCARTE), DRAINED

Makes 10 gildas   Curve a piparra pepper into a C shape and skewer it onto a cocktail pick. Next, encircle one of the olives with an anchovy and slide them onto the pick, so that the anchovy and olive are held in place together. Repeat with the remaining peppers, olives, and anchovies.

Savory Anchovy & Tarragon Shortbread

RECIPE BY
**ANNA
HARRINGTON**

Fish and cookies may seem like an incongruous duo, but I've been hooked on the idea of savory anchovy shortbread since Anna Harrington, the founder of a cookie company called the Rounds, shared her recipe a few years ago with *TASTE*, where I used to be an editor. Anna makes a variety of savory shortbreads, bringing together flavor combinations like curry and cashew, Gruyère and date, and Parmesan and olive. In my riff on her anchovy and green onion shortbread, the tarragon delivers a gentle, anise-like sweetness, which softens the intensity of the salty fish. Since these shortbreads can be made a few days ahead of time, they're a great party trick, host gift, or salty snack to have around for an early evening aperitivo.

½ CUP PLUS 1 TBSP [128 G] SALTED BUTTER, AT ROOM TEMPERATURE

4 ANCHOVY FILLETS IN OLIVE OIL, MINCED

2 TBSP MINCED FRESH TARRAGON LEAVES

2 TBSP MINCED GREEN ONION (GREEN PART ONLY)

¼ TSP FRESHLY GROUND BLACK PEPPER

¼ TSP FLAKY SEA SALT

1 TBSP SUGAR

1 CUP [140 G] ALL-PURPOSE FLOUR

Makes 30 cookies   In a medium bowl, combine the butter, anchovies, tarragon, green onion, black pepper, salt, and sugar, and beat with a wooden spoon until thoroughly mixed and there are no lumps of butter. Stir in the flour and continue stirring until well combined with the butter mixture.

Working over a sheet of wax paper, form the dough into a log about 1½ in [4 cm] in diameter and 7 in [17 cm] long. Roll it up in the wax paper and place inside a ziplock bag or plastic container, or wrap it in foil. Refrigerate for at least 2 hours, and as long as 24 hours.

con't

Preheat the oven to 350°F [180°C]. Line two baking sheets with parchment paper.

Remove the dough from the refrigerator, and using a sharp, clean knife, slice into ¼ in [6 mm] thick rounds. You should wind up with about thirty rounds. Space out the rounds on the baking sheets so that they are at least ½ in [13 mm] apart.

Bake for 25 to 30 minutes, rotating the pans halfway through baking and swapping their positions in the oven, until the cookies' outside edges start to turn very light brown. Transfer to a rack to cool. Serve immediately, or store at room temperature in ziplock bags or tightly closed plastic containers for up to 4 days.

Spicy Sardine Toasts
with Caramelized Shallot & Fennel Jam

Fennel and sardines get along famously. The sweet-salty combination is what makes a classic pasta con le sarde (pasta with sardines) so harmonious. A few ribbons of shaved fennel tossed with lemon and parsley are a welcome accompaniment to any snack board involving canned fish. And when the fennel is caramelized alongside some shallots, it transforms into a dark, sweet jam, which offers the perfect sultry backdrop for a few silvery sardine fillets.

These toasts make a great lunch on their own for two people, but you could also swap in some baguette rounds for the slices of sourdough and turn them into bite-size party fare.

4 SLICES GOOD SOURDOUGH BREAD

1 TBSP BUTTER

1 RECIPE CARAMELIZED SHALLOT & FENNEL JAM (PAGE 47)

ONE 4.2 OZ [120 G] CAN SARDINES IN OLIVE OIL WITH PEPPERS (SUCH AS MATIZ SPICY SARDINES), DRAINED

FENNEL FRONDS, FOR GARNISH

KOSHER SALT AND FRESHLY GROUND BLACK PEPPER

Makes 4 toasts   Toast the bread until it's warmed through and just slightly crisp on the surface, but not brittle. Or place the slices on a baking sheet under the broiler for about 1 minute, rearranging the slices if they start to brown. Spread each piece with some of the butter and a generous spoonful of the shallot jam. Top each toast with a sardine, a few fennel fronds, and a sprinkle of salt and pepper.

Clams

with Spicy Tomato Vinaigrette

When you get your hands on a tin of really special clams or cockles, it's best not to fuss with them too much. Cooking them can turn the delicate texture rubbery and distract from their naturally soft salinity. But serving them over a shallow pool of fresh tomato vinaigrette actually brings out these qualities, rounding out the oceanic flavors with a juicy dose of acidity. Making a tomato vinaigrette isn't much more complicated than grating a really ripe tomato and spiking it with sherry vinegar and olive oil. A good dose of black pepper and a sprinkle of celery leaves make the snack as bracingly refreshing as a good, spicy Clamato Bloody Mary.

1 MEDIUM (ABOUT 7 OZ [200 G]) VERY RIPE HEIRLOOM OR BEEFSTEAK TOMATO

1½ TSP SHERRY VINEGAR

1 TBSP OLIVE OIL

KOSHER SALT AND FRESHLY GROUND BLACK PEPPER

PINCH OF RED PEPPER FLAKES

ONE 4 OZ [115 G] CAN REALLY GOOD CLAMS OR COCKLES (SUCH AS DONOSTIA, MATIZ, CABO DE PEÑAS, OR CONSERVAS DE CAMBADOS)

8 CELERY LEAVES

Serves 2 In a medium bowl, use the large holes on a box grater or metal cheese grater to grate the tomato to a pulp. Discard any large pieces of skin and work your way around the core so that you're grating only the juiciest parts of the tomato. Give the remaining core a squeeze, and discard.

Stir in the vinegar and olive oil, and season with the salt, pepper, and red pepper flakes, keeping in mind that the clams will be very salty. Ladle the tomato vinaigrette into a shallow dish. Drain the liquid from the clams (reserve the brine for your next Bloody Mary or seafood risotto) and lay the clams across the surface of the vinaigrette. Garnish with the celery leaves and a final grind of black pepper.

Pan-Fried Sardines
with Salsa Verde

There are very few meals that wouldn't benefit from an emerald burst of garlicky salsa verde. Grilled steak? Roasted branzino? The egg sandwich that you made while hungover? This acidic, salty green sauce can always step in and save the day if you have a few handfuls of green herbs and a blender. This take, made with parsley, cilantro, capers, and lemon juice, is a particularly cooling complement to oily sardines, especially when they've been lightly panfried so they're warmed through and their skin is slightly crackly.

1 LARGE HANDFUL (¾ OZ [20 G]) FRESH FLAT-LEAF PARSLEY LEAVES

1 MEDIUM HANDFUL (½ OZ [15 G]) FRESH CILANTRO LEAVES

2 TBSP CAPERS

1 GARLIC CLOVE

JUICE OF 1 LEMON

¼ CUP PLUS 1 TBSP [75 ML] OLIVE OIL

KOSHER SALT (OPTIONAL)

ONE 3 TO 4 OZ [85 TO 115 G] CAN SARDINES IN OLIVE OIL (SUCH AS MATIZ, FISHWIFE, BELA, OR NURI), UNDRAINED

Serves 2   In a blender (or in a jar with an immersion blender), combine the parsley, cilantro, capers, garlic, lemon juice, and olive oil. Pulse for about 30 seconds to 1 minute, until the sauce has the consistency of pesto. You can taste for seasoning at this point, but I usually hold back with the salt because the capers, and the sardines you will be eating with the sauce, pack a salty punch. Pour the salsa verde into a shallow bowl or a rimmed plate.

Heat a small skillet over medium heat and pour the oil from the sardines into it. When the oil is hot, about 1 minute, gently place each sardine into the skillet (I do this by hand in order to keep them intact). Cook for about 2 minutes on each side, flipping the sardines over gently, until slightly browned. With a spatula or slotted spoon, carefully transfer the sardines to the prepared bed of salsa verde. Eat while warm.

Vanilla Butter

with Cantabrian Anchovies

RECIPE BY

ALEX RAIJ

Chef Alex Raij is one of the most enthusiastic spokespeople for tinned fish on the planet, especially when it comes to salty, meaty Basque and Cantabrian anchovies. I still think about a meal I had years ago at her Brooklyn restaurant, Saint Julivert, which featured a pristine half-moon of cold vanilla butter served with a few long, languid, glossy anchovy fillets. This may seem like an unlikely pairing, but the vanilla brings a mellow, floral quality, which moderates the fish's intense saltiness. Spread some of the butter on a slice of sourdough with an anchovy on top, and you have something better than the best vanilla cupcake.

4 TBSP [55 G] SALTED BUTTER, AT ROOM TEMPERATURE

1 VANILLA BEAN

¼ TSP SUGAR

1 TBSP OLIVE OIL

ONE 1½ TO 1¾ OZ [40 TO 50 G] TIN GREAT QUALITY CANTABRIAN ANCHOVIES (SUCH AS YURRITA, CODESA, OR DON BOCARTE), DRAINED

SOURDOUGH BREAD, FOR SERVING

Serves 2 to 4   Put the butter in a small bowl. Cut the vanilla bean in half and scrape the seeds onto the butter. Add the sugar, and mix until the vanilla flecks are evenly distributed and the sugar has dissolved slightly, about 1 minute.

Line a small ring mold or a round 1 pt [475 ml] plastic deli container with plastic wrap and spread the butter across the bottom in an even layer. Cover and refrigerate for at least 1 hour.

When you're ready to serve, carefully unmold the butter onto a cutting board, and cut in half. Rewrap one half in the plastic wrap and refrigerate for your next anchovy snack or to spread on toast in the morning. Set the other half on a round plate and drizzle the olive oil onto the empty half. Set the anchovy fillets across the diameter of the plate, dividing the butter side from the olive oil side. Serve with the bread.

Smoked Mackerel Onigiri

I will probably never get sick of eating convenience store onigiri, straight out of the refrigerator case and stuffed full of canned tuna mixed with spicy mayo. But making these rice balls at home has a few strong advantages. For one, you get to eat them while the rice is warm, the grains sticking together gently but not yet solidified into place. Second, you can experiment with different fillings and mix-ins. Here they take the form of smoked mackerel (I encourage you to try these with other types of oily fish, too!), thinly sliced green onion, and furikake. The rice warms each flake of fish, and in return, the fish seasons each grain of rice with its salty, flavorful oil.

1 CUP [210 G] SHORT-GRAIN SUSHI RICE

ONE 4 OZ [115 G] CAN SMOKED MACKEREL FILLETS (SUCH AS PATAGONIA), DRAINED

1 TSP SOY SAUCE

¼ TSP SESAME OIL

2 GREEN ONIONS (WHITE AND GREEN PARTS), THINLY SLICED

1 TBSP FURIKAKE

SIX 1½ BY 3½ IN [4 BY 9 CM] STRIPS NORI

KOSHER SALT

Makes 6 onigiri   Rinse the rice under cold running water until the water runs clear. Cook the rice in a rice cooker or on a stove top, according to the instructions on the package. Meanwhile, in a small bowl, use a fork to flake apart the mackerel fillets, and stir in the soy sauce and sesame oil. With the rice cooker paddle or a wooden spatula, gently fold the mackerel mixture, green onions, and furikake into the finished rice.

Set up a workstation for yourself with the stack of nori, a medium bowl of warm water, and a small dish of salt. Dip your hands in the water and sprinkle a bit of salt onto the palm of each hand. Gather a handful of rice and gently form it into a triangle with 2 in [2 cm] sides and rounded edges, squeezing just enough for the rice to hold together. Lay the base of the triangle of rice in the middle of a strip of nori and wrap the ends of the nori around the rice. Repeat with the remaining rice and nori. Serve while warm.

THE ANATOMY OF A PERFECT TINNED FISH PLATE

A great tin of fish wouldn't be out of place on a cheeseboard or charcuterie board, but why not make the fish the star of the show? Some of the best parties and picnics I've hosted have involved picking out five or six tins from my cupboard and building a snack spread around them. Everyone winds up trying something new, including me. And setting out the right variety of pickles, olives, chips, and crackers means that every bite is different from the last. Whether you're hosting twenty-five people on a Friday night or putting together a civilized work-from-home lunch, consider adding . . .

SOMETHING ACIDIC

Most canned seafood has a pretty mellow, mild flavor when you crack open the tin, even when preserved with lemon or spices. That's why it's great to serve something citrusy or pickled alongside. This could mean a few lemon wedges or a ramekin of Lemon Confit (page 45). It's also a great opportunity to pull out some juicy green Castelvetrano olives, cornichons, or Pickled Shallots (page 44).

SOMETHING BREADY

For a small gathering or a simple dinner at home, I

love breaking into a crusty baguette or sourdough loaf to eat with tinned fish. For a party or picnic, nothing's easier, breezier, or crunchier than a stack of saltines or Triscuits, or a bag of sturdy potato chips.

SOMETHING CREAMY

Butter is the absolute MVP of the tinned fish plate. The light tang of a cultured butter plays perfectly with salty sardines, but there are also plenty of compound butters, like Nori Butter (page 53), that are great matches for small, oily fish. To serve with tinned octopus, mussels, or oysters, try a faintly garlicky aioli, like Saffron Aioli (page 52).

SOMETHING FRESH

If you've read this far, you know that you could put together a pretty great party from your pantry on the spur of the moment. But when you do have time to plan a little, adding a refreshing, crunchy, herbaceous element can carry your snack array into professional territory. This could mean crudités, like cucumbers, cherry tomatoes, fennel, and blanched asparagus, or the Perfectly Dressed Herb Salad (page 57).

SOMETHING SPICY

There are few accompaniments for smoked mussels or oysters that are better than a bottle of hot sauce. Or try a small pile of piparras (pickled guindilla peppers) to go with sardines, mackerel, and other oily fish, or a sprinkle of paprika on those delicate, briny clams.

Quick-Pickled Mussels
with Carrots & Tarragon

Mussels are one of the most sustainable types of seafood, and they're packed with protein, vitamin B_{12}, and iron. Tinned mussels have still more advantages: They can transport you to a Parisian bistro with a quick pop of the lid, and they have a much more tender, less elastic texture than the freshly steamed variety. Adding some vinegar, grated garlic, and fresh herbs is a quick way to turn the contents of the can into a fancy snack, to be served alongside a shot glass full of toothpicks.

1 SMALL GARLIC CLOVE, GRATED

2 TBSP RED WINE VINEGAR

2 TBSP OLIVE OIL

½ TSP SUGAR

½ SMALL SHALLOT, MINCED

ONE 4 OZ [115 G] CAN SMOKED MUSSELS IN BROTH (SUCH AS PATAGONIA), UNDRAINED

2 SMALL CARROTS, PEELED AND DICED

4 SPRIGS FRESH TARRAGON LEAVES, FINELY CHOPPED, PLUS 5 OR 6 LEAVES FOR GARNISH

FRESHLY GROUND BLACK PEPPER

Serves 4   In a small bowl, whisk together the garlic, vinegar, olive oil, sugar, and shallot. Add the mussels and about 1 Tbsp of the broth from the can. Add the carrots and chopped tarragon, season with black pepper, and toss gently.

Cover and marinate in the refrigerator for at least 30 minutes, or as long as 24 hours. Serve in a small glass bowl (an ice-cream bowl or champagne coupe is fun for this) garnished with the tarragon leaves, with some toothpicks for spearing the mussels and carrots.

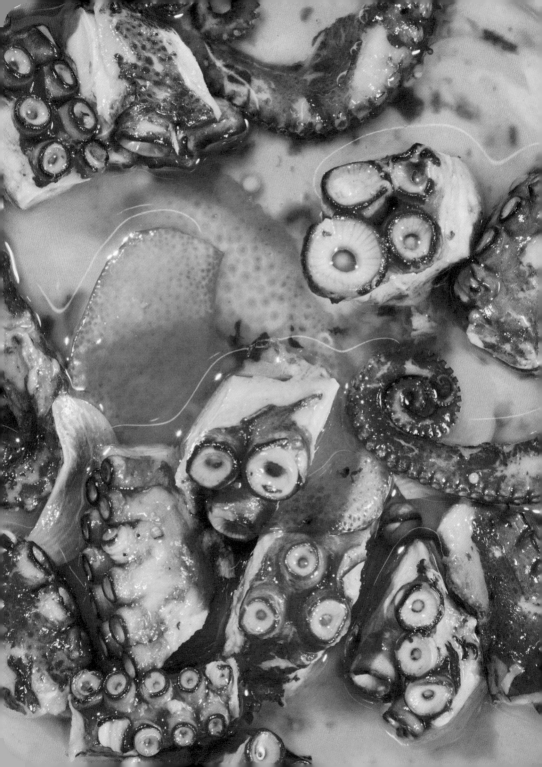

Octopus

Marinated with Chili Powder & Orange Peel

Octopus packed in olive oil is one of the most luxurious treats you can buy in a tin for less than the cost of a glass of wine. The best tins contain perfectly portioned, bite-size pieces of tender, glossy purple octopus meat in a savory oil. These don't need much tinkering to taste great, but I like to give them a quick warm bath in some garlicky, subtly spiced olive oil. The oil melds with the liquid from the can and a splash of fresh citrus and vinegar to create a broth you'll want to eat by the spoonful, or at least sop up with the heel of a baguette.

2 TBSP OLIVE OIL

1 GARLIC CLOVE, THINLY SLICED

2 RIBBONS ORANGE ZEST

¼ TSP PIMENT D'ESPELETTE OR PAPRIKA

ONE 4 OZ [115 G] CAN OCTOPUS IN OLIVE OIL, UNDRAINED

½ TSP FRESH ORANGE JUICE

½ TSP WHITE WINE VINEGAR OR SHERRY VINEGAR

BAGUETTE, FOR SERVING

Serves 2   In a small skillet over medium-low heat, warm the olive oil, garlic, orange zest, and piment d'Espelette. Sauté gently for about 4 minutes, until the garlic is tender.

Remove from the heat and add the whole can of octopus, with its liquid. Add the orange juice and vinegar. Toss to coat and warm the octopus, and serve immediately with the baguette.

Vermouth Hour Potato Chips

with Mussels, Olives & Piparras

In Catalonia, some of the most important staples for an afternoon snack are potato chips, pickled things, and a good house vermouth served on ice with a wedge of orange and a green olive. One of my favorite places to enjoy this particular combination is at Morro Fi, in Barcelona. The tiny bar makes its own vermouth and patates amb musclos i seitons, freshly fried thick-cut potato chips, topped with your pick of marinated mussels, vinegary boquerónes (lightly pickled anchovies), salt-cured anchovies, and olives. This dish is an ode to these tasty morsels.

ONE 5 OZ [140 G] BAG STURDY SALTED POTATO CHIPS (SUCH AS KETTLE, BONILLA A LA VISTA, OR FOX FAMILY)

ONE 4 OZ [115 G] TIN MUSSELS IN ESCABECHE (SUCH AS DONOSTIA, RAMÓN PEÑA, LA BRÚJULA, OR CABO DE PEÑAS), DRAINED

6 CASTELVETRANO OLIVES

6 PIPARRAS (PICKLED GUINDILLA PEPPERS)

½ TSP ESPINALER APPETIZER SAUCE, OR ½ TSP WHITE WINE VINEGAR MIXED WITH A PINCH OF PAPRIKA

Serves 4   Spread the chips out in a medium shallow bowl. Top with the mussels, olives, and piparras. Sprinkle with the appetizer sauce or vinegar and serve.

Smoked Salmon Deviled Eggs
with Black Sesame Seeds

The vibe here is a little like a sesame bagel piled high with beet-cured lox and red onion. With a few Beet-Pickled Eggs (page 120) in your refrigerator, the perfect afternoon snack or platter of sophisticated hors d'oeuvres is just a few minutes away. I like to use Scout smoked wild pink salmon, Fishwife smoked Atlantic salmon, or Wildfish Cannery smoked king salmon here. These are great with a glass of sparkling wine and even better alongside some potato chips and caviar.

1 RECIPE BEET-PICKLED EGGS (PAGE 120)

2 TBSP MAYONNAISE

1 TBSP MINCED SHALLOT

1 TBSP CHAMPAGNE VINEGAR

½ TSP DIJON MUSTARD

⅛ TSP FRESHLY GROUND BLACK PEPPER

ONE 3½ OZ [100 G] TIN SMOKED SALMON, DRAINED

TINY SPRIGS OF FRESH DILL, FOR GARNISH

BLACK SESAME SEEDS OR EVERYTHING BAGEL SEASONING, FOR GARNISH

Makes 12 deviled egg halves   Using a sharp knife, cut each egg in half lengthwise, wiping the knife with a damp paper towel between cuts. Use a small spoon to scoop the yolks into a medium bowl and arrange the whites on a serving plate.

To the yolks, add the mayonnaise, shallot, vinegar, mustard, and black pepper. Add half the salmon from the can. Use an immersion blender or hand mixer to blend together until it has emulsified into a uniform mixture. (Alternatively, whisk vigorously with a fork—you just won't achieve quite as creamy a texture.) Use two small spoons (or a piping bag) to scoop an equal amount of the yolk mixture into each egg white half.

Gently flake the remaining salmon and garnish each egg half with a piece of fish. Garnish each one with a sprig of dill and a sprinkle of sesame seeds or everything bagel seasoning. Serve immediately or cover with plastic wrap and refrigerate for up to 4 hours.

Beet-Pickled Eggs

Pickled eggs may seem like a bygone bar snack to some, but to me, they're a shortcut to glamorous hors d'oeuvres, like the Smoked Salmon Deviled Eggs with Black Sesame Seeds (page 119) and vibrant salads, like the Everything Pink Salad (page 143). The addition of a beet to the pickling liquid adds a soft, natural sweetness and turns the egg whites an eye-catching shade of magenta. The creamy texture of the egg, paired with the sweet and sour punch of vinegar, is a perfect foil for a whole range of tinned fishes, including trout, herring, and anchovies.

1 MEDIUM BEET, TRIMMED AND QUARTERED

⅓ CUP [65 G] SUGAR

⅓ CUP [80 ML] DISTILLED WHITE VINEGAR

6 BLACK PEPPERCORNS

PINCH OF KOSHER SALT

1 BAY LEAF

6 EGGS

Makes 6 eggs In a medium saucepan, combine the beet, sugar, vinegar, peppercorns, salt, and bay leaf with 2 cups [480 ml] of water. Bring to a simmer over medium-low heat and cook for 20 minutes. Remove from the heat and let cool to room temperature.

Meanwhile, bring another medium saucepan with 3 in [7.5 cm] of water to a boil over medium heat. Add the eggs and cook for exactly 8 minutes. Remove from the heat, remove the eggs from the pan, and rinse the eggs with cold water to stop their cooking.

Peel the eggs and transfer to a 1 qt [945 ml] plastic container or wide-mouth glass jar with a tight-fitting cover. Pour in the beet liquid. If it does not cover the eggs completely, add a splash or two of water. Cover and refrigerate for at least 2 hours. The eggs will keep for up to 2 days.

Deviled Eggs

with Pickled Mussels

One of the most luxurious treats you can buy in a can is mussels in escabeche. Each jewel-like mussel is bathed in a Spanish oil-and-vinegar marinade, tinted red with paprika and full of garlic and warm spices like nutmeg, clove, or cinnamon. The vinaigrette (also sometimes labeled "mussels in olive oil and vinegar" or "mussels in pickled sauce") is delicious enough to drink. For these deviled eggs, the marinade is used to infuse the egg yolk filling with plenty of umami, acidity, and spice.

6 EGGS

1½ TSP MINCED SHALLOT

1 TBSP MAYONNAISE

ONE 4 OZ [115 G] CAN MUSSELS IN ESCABECHE (SUCH AS DONOSTIA, MATIZ, OR RAMÓN PEÑA), UNDRAINED

¼ TSP SHERRY VINEGAR, PLUS MORE AS NEEDED

1 TSP MINCED FRESH CHIVES, FOR GARNISH

PINCH OF PAPRIKA, PLUS MORE AS NEEDED, FOR GARNISH

Makes 12 deviled egg halves Fill a medium pot with 3 in [7.5 cm] of water and bring to a boil. Using a ladle or a large spoon, gently lower the eggs into the boiling water, one by one, and cook for exactly 9 minutes. Drain the eggs, rinse briefly with cold water, and peel.

Cut each egg in half lengthwise. Use a small spoon to scoop the yolks into a medium bowl and transfer the egg white halves to a serving plate. Add the minced shallot, mayonnaise, and 2 Tbsp of the pickling liquid from the can of mussels to the bowl with the egg yolks. Use a hand mixer or immersion blender to mix until creamy. Mix in the vinegar and paprika, and taste, adding more of each if necessary.

Use two small spoons (or a piping bag) to scoop an equal amount of the yolk mixture into each egg white half. Garnish each with a mussel, a pinch of the chives, and a dusting of paprika. Serve immediately or cover with plastic wrap and refrigerate for up to 4 hours.

3

SALADS

Any salad can be a tinned fish salad if you happen to open a tin at the right moment. And most piles of green, leafy vegetables would benefit from some fortifying, sparkling sardines or a few flaky fillets of mackerel. But when used wisely, a good tin of fish can bring much more to your salads than pure convenience or protein.

Oil-packed tuna can be whizzed into a silky, creamy tonnato sauce that clings to the folds in a radicchio leaf. Anchovies can offer a salty foil to the sweet, toasty flavor of challah bread crumbs on a Caesar salad. And trout can lend a dose of sultry smoke to a mix of bitter Castelfranco and sweet Beet-Pickled Eggs (page 120).

There's no wrong time of the day or year to pair a tin with some crisp greens, but the recipes in this chapter will give you a few ideas for eating your way through the seasons, whether you're looking for midweek work-from-home lunches or dinner party centerpieces.

Little Gems Caesar
with Challah Bread Crumbs & Black Sesame

To me, the best surprise upon ordering a Caesar salad at a restaurant is discovering that the croutons have been made with a sesame loaf. You get that warm, nutty toasted sesame flavor, which contrasts so sharply with the cool, creamy dressing. But I like croutons made with sweet, eggy, rich challah almost as much. This Caesar combines the best of both worlds: the challah bread crumbs are toasted with a few meaty anchovy fillets and a generous spoonful of black sesame seeds, which add a beautiful visual contrast to the bright green Little Gems (a smaller, more tender alternative to romaine). And even better, between the dressing and the bread crumbs, this salad uses up an entire tin of anchovies, so you won't be left with any odds and ends in your refrigerator.

1 THICK SLICE CHALLAH

3 HEADS LITTLE GEM LETTUCE

1½ TBSP OLIVE OIL

5 ANCHOVY FILLETS

1½ TSP BLACK SESAME SEEDS

PINCH OF KOSHER SALT

1 RECIPE LEMONY CAESAR DRESSING (PAGE 65)

½ CUP [15 G] GRATED PARMESAN CHEESE

Serves 4 to 6   Preheat the oven to 200°F [95°C]. Carefully (without smooshing the bread too much) break the slices of challah into small, bite-size pieces, and spread them out on a baking sheet. Toast in the oven for about 15 minutes, or until they feel dry and brittle to the touch. Let cool.

Meanwhile, trim off the very bottoms of the cores from the heads of lettuce and cut each head in half. Rinse carefully (trying not to separate the leaves), and pat dry with a dish towel. Let sit, cut-side down, on the dish towel to continue drying.

con't

Put the challah pieces in a blender or food processor and pulse for about 30 seconds, or until they have been reduced to bread crumbs (it's okay if there are a few larger, irregular-sized pieces).

In a small skillet over low heat, heat the olive oil with the anchovies, using a spatula to stir the anchovies into the oil and break them up slightly. Add the bread crumbs and sesame seeds. Fry for about 5 minutes, stirring constantly with a spatula, until the bread crumbs have darkened in color and start to smell fragrant. Transfer to a small bowl.

Give the lettuce halves a final pat dry and transfer to a large mixing bowl. Drizzle the dressing into the bowl slowly, while using tongs to gently toss the lettuce halves, coating them with the dressing. Arrange the lettuce on a platter, cut-side up, and drizzle any left-over dressing into the spaces between the leaves.

Sprinkle the lettuce with the Parmesan and ½ cup [50 g] of the bread crumbs, and serve immediately. Store any leftover bread crumbs in a sealed container in the refrigerator and use within three days.

Grilled Radicchio
with Fresh Tomatoes & Tonnato

Radicchio is bracingly bitter and admirably hardy, which means two things: It can tolerate the intense heat of a grill, and it can stand up to a creamy, salty dressing. I love grilling radicchio because it softens those tougher outer leaves ever so slightly, and the char flavor plays perfectly with the bitterness, but you can also give it a quick roast in the oven. This salad would be a great, unexpected side to serve with grilled steak or chicken quarters.

2 SMALL HEADS RADICCHIO

1 TSP OLIVE OIL

½ CUP [120 ML] TONNATO SAUCE (PAGE 63)

3 SMALL HEIRLOOM TOMATOES (1⅓ LB [600 G]) OF VARIOUS COLORS

1 RECIPE CRISPY FRIED CAPERS (PAGE 58), FOR GARNISH

2 TBSP SMALL FRESH BASIL LEAVES, FOR GARNISH

FLAKY SEA SALT AND FRESHLY GROUND BLACK PEPPER

Serves 4 to 8 Preheat the grill for indirect, medium heat. Or preheat the oven to 500°F [260°C]. Cut the heads of radicchio into quarters, rinse, and pat dry with a dish towel. Transfer to a medium bowl. Add the olive oil and use your hands to toss the radicchio with the oil.

Place the radicchio on the grill, or on a baking sheet in the oven, and cook for 5 to 7 minutes, flipping them halfway through, until the flat, cut surfaces are lightly charred and the leaves are tender but still have some structure and crunch. Remove from the heat.

Spread about half the tonnato sauce across the surface of a large serving platter. Using tongs, gently arrange the radicchio in the center. Cut the tomatoes in half from end to end, and then cut each half into thirds. Arrange the tomato wedges around the radicchio. Drizzle the rest of the tonnato sauce over the vegetables, and garnish with the fried capers and basil leaves. Season with salt and pepper.

RECIPE BY
MANSOUR AREM

S'han Tounsi

with Mokli (Tunisian Plate with Fried Eggs)

One of my favorite accompaniments to a rich, oil-packed tuna is the velvety, fruity, nuanced harissa of Zwïta, a Houston-based company founded by Tunisian-American brothers Mansour and Karim Arem. Zwïta's harissa is made with the type of careful craftsmanship and intentional sourcing that many of my favorite tins of fish are produced with, and when it's combined with one of those tins, both ingredients shine even brighter.

Mansour generously shared with me his recipe for a Tunisian staple called S'han Tounsi, which translates literally to "Tunisian plate." The exact makeup of the dish varies slightly, depending on who's making it, but it brings together a symphony of briny olives, poached or fried eggs, verdant fresh vegetables, salty tuna, and raisin-y harissa, making each bite slightly different from the last.

Mansour takes a cue from his mother and incorporates fried eggs and a few juicy fried tomatoes and peppers (all typical elements of a mokli, or "fried plate") into his version, for a balance of cooked and raw elements. While it takes a bit of work to assemble each component, the finished dish is well worth it, especially when you taste the way a bite of tuna can be improved by this symphony of flavors and textures.

con't

1 PERSIAN CUCUMBER (OR ½ SMALL CUCUMBER)

3 PLUM TOMATOES

¼ RED ONION

1 TSP RED WINE VINEGAR

2 TSP FRESH LEMON JUICE

1 TSP PLUS ½ CUP [120 ML] OLIVE OIL

PINCH OF DRIED MINT

KOSHER SALT AND FRESHLY GROUND BLACK PEPPER

4 SMALL YUKON GOLD POTATOES

1 TSP MINCED FRESH FLAT-LEAF PARSLEY

4 SMALL GARLIC CLOVES

2 LONG, SKINNY CHILES, SUCH AS ANAHEIM CHILES, BANANA PEPPERS, OR ITALIAN LONG HOTS

2 EGGS

ONE 5 OZ [140 G] CAN TUNA IN OLIVE OIL, DRAINED

16 TO 18 OLIVES, SUCH AS KALAMATA OR GAETA

2 TBSP HARISSA

BAGUETTE, FOR SERVING

Serves 2   First, make the slata Tounsia (Tunisian salad). Dice the cucumber, one tomato, and the red onion into small cubes. In a medium bowl, toss with the vinegar, 1 tsp of the lemon juice, 1 tsp of the olive oil, the dried mint, a pinch of salt, and a few grinds of black pepper. Set aside.

Put the potatoes in a small saucepan with a pinch of salt and cover with water. Place over medium heat, bring to a boil, and cook at a gentle boil until a fork spears the potatoes easily, about 20 minutes. Drain the potatoes and let sit until cool enough to handle. Slice the potatoes ¼ in [6 mm] thick. Transfer to a medium bowl, add the remaining 1 tsp of lemon juice, the parsley, and a pinch of salt. Set aside.

Cut the remaining 2 tomatoes in half, wedge 1 clove of garlic into the center of each half, and sprinkle generously with salt. Set aside. Cut the chiles in half lengthwise and salt the insides.

In a medium skillet, heat the remaining ½ cup [120 ml] of olive oil over medium-low heat until it begins to shimmer. Put the chiles in the oil, skin-side down, and cook for about 5 minutes, or until the skin becomes slightly wrinkled and the flesh softens. Use a pair of tongs to flip them over, and fry on the other side for 5 minutes more. Drain on a paper towel–lined plate.

Add the tomato halves to the hot oil, skin-side down. Cook for about 30 minutes, flipping every 8 minutes, until the tomato is slightly shriveled and has turned a rich, dark red color. Transfer to a plate.

Drain off all but 2 Tbsp of the oil from the skillet. (The drained oil is full of sweet, concentrated tomato flavor, so set it aside in a glass jar for dipping bread, or to use in a vinaigrette.)

Crack the eggs into the hot skillet and cover with a lid. Cook over medium-low heat for about 2 minutes, or until the egg white is set and the egg yolk is still creamy.

Transfer the eggs to the center of a serving plate, and surround them with the slata Tounsia, potatoes, fried peppers and tomatoes, tuna, olives, and harissa. Serve with the bread.

FUSSY SALAD NIGHT

One of my most time-honored personal cooking traditions is a little ritual I like to call Fussy Salad Night. About one night a week, I give myself the challenge of making a salad for dinner that I would be willing to pay for in a fancy restaurant. When I play my cards right, the salad pairs a few raw ingredients with a few thoughtfully cooked ingredients, and enough protein to count as a real meal. More often than not, there's canned fish involved.

The real key here is to dress the greens first and then transfer them to a big platter, or directly onto your dinner plate, where they become a bed for the other ingredients. This will ensure that all of the flavors and textures are distributed evenly, and the crispy toppings will stay crispy, rather than falling to the bottom of the pile and getting soggy. Here are a few more tips for constructing your own salad masterpiece.

SOMETHING LEAFY AND DRESSED

Personally, I love a green with some structure, like Little Gems, romaine, or radicchio. Try a dressing with a simple French vinaigrette like My Go-To Vinaigrette (page 64) or something a little creamier, like the Lemony Caesar Dressing (page 65).

SOMETHING SUBSTANTIAL

This can be the leftover half of a roast chicken in your refrigerator or a good hunk of Roquefort, but I love the combo of a jammy egg or a Beet-Pickled Egg (page 120) and a can of fish. Oily fish like mackerel, sardines, and anchovies can add richness if you're dressing your salad with a lighter vinaigrette, and salmon or trout can add smokiness, instead of bacon.

SOMETHING CRUNCHY

I love the way something really crunchy, like radishes, sugar snap peas, or cucumber, complement tender lettuce leaves.

SOMETHING CRISPY

Think carrots roasted to a crisp, fried shallots, sesame seeds, candied pistachios, or Crispy Fried Capers (page 58).

Marinated French Lentil & Smoked Trout Salad

Meal prep can be daunting. But nothing creates the illusion of sophistication and having your shit together like cooking a pot of lentils at the beginning of the week and marinating them in a French-ish, mustardy vinaigrette. With some smoky tinned trout and crispy mushrooms, this salad has become a deeply satisfying year-round standby.

1 CUP [200 G] FRENCH LENTILS

3 TBSP MY GO-TO VINAIGRETTE (PAGE 64)

1 BUNCH GREEN ONIONS, ENDS TRIMMED AND ANY BROWN OR DRY OUTER LAYERS REMOVED

8 OZ [230 G] BABY BELLA MUSHROOMS, RUBBED CLEAN OF DIRT AND THICKLY SLICED

1 SPRIG FRESH THYME (OPTIONAL)

1 TBSP OLIVE OIL

¼ TSP KOSHER SALT

1 TSP RED WINE VINEGAR

ONE 3 TO 4 OZ [85 TO 115 G] TIN SMOKED TROUT (SUCH AS TRADER JOE'S, FISHWIFE, COLE'S, OR JOSE GOURMET), DRAINED AND FLAKED IN A FEW LARGE PIECES

Serves 2   Preheat the oven to 425°F [220°C].

Fill a medium pot with water and bring to a boil over high heat. Add the lentils, lower the heat, and simmer for about 25 minutes, until al dente. Drain and let cool until just slightly warm. Transfer to a medium bowl, toss them with the vinaigrette, and give them a few minutes to soak it up.

Meanwhile, cut the green onions in half lengthwise and then crosswise into 2 in [5 cm] segments. Transfer to a baking sheet. Add the mushrooms, thyme, and olive oil, and toss together. Sprinkle with the salt and roast, stirring every 5 minutes, for about 15 minutes, or until the moisture from the mushrooms has cooked off, and the green onions and mushrooms are beginning to turn brown. Sprinkle the vinegar over the vegetables and stir to incorporate. Return to the oven for 10 more minutes, or until the mushrooms and green onions are slightly crispy around the edges.

Divide the lentils between two plates and top with the trout, mushrooms, and green onions.

Mac & Mack

Macaroni are the fun, easygoing kings of the pasta world. These short, bendy noodles are experts in absorbing dressing and in gently curling around crunchy vegetables and fresh herbs, which makes them perfect for cold pasta salads, like this lemony mackerel and white bean salad. The salad might be distantly related to the mayo-laden tuna and pasta salads my mom used to make when I was a kid, but it's brighter and more herby and peppery. Packed with protein, it makes a deeply satisfying lunch on its own, but it would also make waves at a potluck.

KOSHER SALT

1 CUP [130 G] ELBOW MACARONI

2 TBSP FRESH LEMON JUICE

1 TBSP PEPPERONCINI BRINE, PLUS 6 SMALL PICKLED PEPPERONCINI, MINCED

1 TSP SUGAR

ONE 3 OZ [85 G] CAN MACKEREL FILLETS IN OLIVE OIL, UNDRAINED

1 CELERY STALK, MINCED

1 SMALL SHALLOT, MINCED

2 TBSP LEMON CONFIT (PAGE 45), MINCED

ONE 15½ OZ [440 G] CAN SMALL WHITE BEANS, DRAINED AND RINSED

2 TBSP MINCED FRESH FLAT-LEAF PARSLEY

1 TBSP MINCED FRESH DILL

FRESHLY GROUND BLACK PEPPER

Serves 4   Fill a medium saucepan two-thirds of the way with water. Add a big pinch of salt, cover, and bring to a boil over medium-high heat. Add the macaroni and cook until al dente, about 6 minutes. Drain in a colander and cool slightly.

Meanwhile, in a small bowl or glass measuring cup, whisk together the lemon juice, pepperoncini brine, and sugar, and add 1 Tbsp of the olive oil from the mackerel tin.

In a medium bowl, use a fork to flake apart the mackerel. Add the celery, shallot, pepperoncini, and lemon confit, and mix thoroughly. Carefully, so as not to smoosh them, fold in the beans, and then the macaroni, lemon juice mixture, parsley, and dill. Season with pepper and, if needed, with salt (the mackerel and pepperoncini brine will both be very salty). Serve immediately, or cover and store in the refrigerator for up to 3 days.

Late-Summer Niçoise
with Fresh Corn & Cherry Tomatoes

The Niçoise salad is a controversial dish to riff on. The good people of Nice would, without a doubt, turn up their noses at this very American celebration of summer produce. But how can I be blamed when August in New York brings such sweet corn, crisp green beans, and ripe tomatoes, which are only made better crowned with a few great oil-packed fillets? Since I'm already in trouble with the French, I'm taking this salad a step further by swapping out the tuna for the delicate, mild flakes of mackerel fillets. But feel free to substitute the tin of your choice—because salad rules are made to be broken.

2 EARS FRESH CORN

1 TSP OLIVE OIL

4 OZ [115 G] GREEN BEANS, ENDS TRIMMED

10 BABY POTATOES OR FINGERLINGS

2 EGGS

1 ROMAINE HEART, LEAVES SEPARATED, WASHED, AND PATTED DRY

3½ OZ [100 G] CHERRY TOMATOES, HALVED

TWO 4 TO 5 OZ [115 TO 140 G] CANS MACKEREL FILLETS (OR TUNA), IN OLIVE OIL, DRAINED

¼ CUP [60 ML] MY GO-TO VINAIGRETTE (PAGE 64)

1 GREEN ONION, THINLY SLICED (GREEN AND WHITE PARTS)

FLAKY SEA SALT AND FRESHLY GROUND BLACK PEPPER

Serves 4 as a side, or 2 as a meal   Preheat the broiler. Husk the ears of corn and rub with the olive oil. Place on a baking sheet and broil for 5 to 8 minutes, rotating every couple of minutes, until the corn is charred all over. Cool slightly and cut the corn kernels off the cobs.

Fill a medium bowl with ice water. Fill a medium saucepan with salted water, bring to a boil, and add the green beans. Cook over medium heat for 5 minutes. With a slotted spoon, transfer to the ice bath for about 5 minutes to stop the cooking, ensuring the green beans remain slightly crunchy, with a vibrant green color. Drain and pat dry.

con't

Add the baby potatoes to the green bean cooking water and cook for about 12 minutes, or until a fork can pierce the potatoes easily. With a slotted spoon, scoop the potatoes out of the water and onto a cutting board. When cool enough to handle, cut each potato in half.

Return the potato cooking water to a boil and add the eggs. Cook for exactly 8 minutes. Drain the eggs, rinse with cold water, and let cool. Peel and cut into quarters.

Arrange the romaine leaves on a large platter. Arrange the potato halves, egg quarters, green beans, cherry tomatoes, corn kernels, and mackerel fillets in clusters on the platter, so they fan out from the center. Drizzle the vinaigrette across the entire platter and sprinkle the vegetables with the green onions. Season with salt and pepper.

Everything Pink Salad
with Castelfranco, Radishes, Beet-Pickled Eggs & Smoked Trout

When the magenta-to-purple spectrum of radicchios are in season, from late fall through early spring, my salad routine becomes increasingly ostentatious. It's a chance to play with their bitter, crisp flavors, and it's also a chance to make a completely monochromatic salad that's anything but boring. This particular salad quadruples down on the pink with Castelfranco (a pale pink, very tender variety of radicchio), watermelon radishes, Beet-Pickled Eggs (page 120), and smoked trout. Even though the display of sunset hues may seem intricate, it's easy enough to pull off for a weekday lunch, if you have a few pickled eggs in the refrigerator.

1 HEAD CASTELFRANCO OR ANOTHER LEAFY, DELICATE RADICCHIO

2 TBSP MY GO-TO VINAIGRETTE (PAGE 64)

1 SMALL WATERMELON RADISH, THINLY SLICED

2 BEET-PICKLED EGGS (PAGE 120)

ONE 4 TO 6 OZ [115 TO 170 G] CAN SMOKED TROUT, DRAINED

1 TBSP MINCED FRESH CHIVES

FLAKY SEA SALT AND FRESHLY GROUND BLACK PEPPER

Serves 2   In a large bowl, toss the Castelfranco leaves with the vinaigrette, using a set of tongs to make sure each leaf is coated. Carefully transfer the dressed lettuce leaves to a large platter, leaving the excess vinaigrette behind in the bowl.

Add the radish to the mixing bowl and use the tongs to toss and coat in the vinaigrette. Arrange the radish slices on the platter with the Castelfranco, again leaving any excess vinaigrette behind in the bowl.

Cut each pickled egg into quarters and arrange them across the serving platter. Drain and discard the oil from the smoked trout, use a fork to break apart the meat, and distribute evenly across the salad. Drizzle any remaining vinaigrette over the entire salad, and sprinkle evenly with the chives. Season with salt and pepper.

4

SANDWICHES

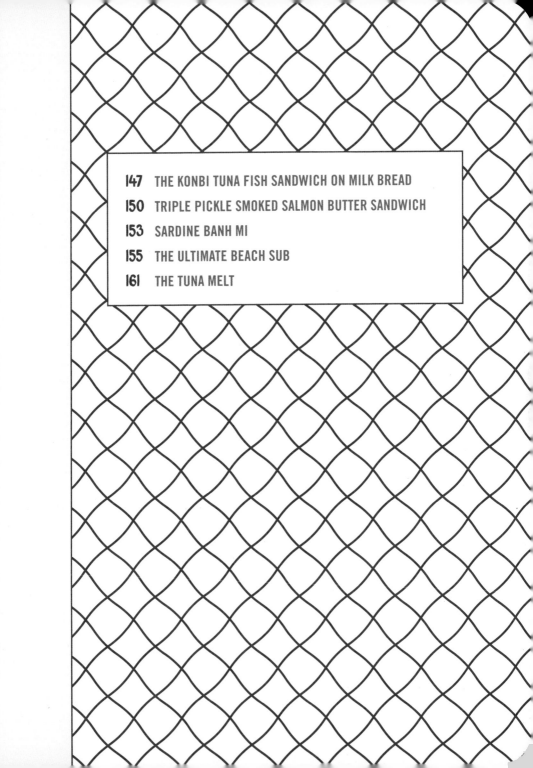

To me, tinned fish is the ultimate fast food. Opening a can is faster and cheaper than placing a delivery order, is quicker than running to the bodega across the street, and will provide you with much more vitamin D than an order of chicken nuggets from a rest stop. And once that tinned fish is tucked into a baguette or between a couple slices of pillowy milk bread, it becomes a convenience food that you can wrap in wax paper and toss into a bag for your busy lunch break, or take along on a hike and enjoy next to a glittering lake.

The sandwiches in this chapter show how much fun it can be to take tinned fish on the go, whether that means an Italian sub that's perfectly built for the beach or a mackerel sandwich that's pretty enough to serve at a picnic. Andrea Nguyen shares her trick for doctoring a tin of sardines in tomato sauce to bring out all of its sweet, salty, bright qualities, making it a perfect protein for a banh mi. There's also a breathtakingly chic take on a convenience store tuna sandwich from Akira Akuto and Nick Montgomery, the owners of Konbi in Los Angeles. And for some New York nostalgia, there's a tuna melt that will hold its own alongside the best egg cream.

The Konbi Tuna Fish Sandwich on Milk Bread

RECIPE BY
NICK MONTGOMERY + AKIRA AKUTO

In addition to their beautifully made pastries, LA's Konbi is famous for their thoughtful reinterpretations of classic Japanese convenience store sandwiches. Packed between slices of milk bread (an especially pillowy take on white bread) are sunny yellow egg salad and perfectly crisp eggplant katsu. But the sandwich on the menu that always catches my eye is the tuna fish sandwich.

In a stroke of tinned fish genius, owners Akira Akuto and Nick Montgomery drain tins of water-packed tuna and marinate them overnight in a combination of mirin and shoyu (light soy sauce). The next day they drain them again and mix it with pickled celery and Kewpie mayonnaise, a Japanese mayo rich in egg yolks. The resulting sandwich looks deceptively simple, but it's layered with flavor and texture. These are best made fresh, to prevent the milk bread (which you might find at your nearest Japanese or Korean bakery) from getting soggy, but consider marinating the tuna, pickling the celery, and prepping the mayo (which is spiked with spicy, citrusy yuzu kosho) the night before.

ONE 5 OZ [140 G] CAN TUNA IN WATER, DRAINED

2 TBSP LIGHT SOY SAUCE

3 TBSP MIRIN

1 SMALL CELERY STALK, THINLY SLICED

⅓ CUP [80 ML] RICE WINE VINEGAR

1 TBSP SUGAR

¼ TSP KOSHER SALT

⅛ SMALL RED ONION, CUT INTO THIN SLIVERS

4 TBSP [60 G] KEWPIE MAYONNAISE

2 TSP AO NORI

¼ TSP YUZU KOSHO

4 SLICES MILK BREAD

ONE 8 IN [20 CM] SEEDLESS CUCUMBER, THINLY SLICED

con't

Makes 2 sandwiches   In a small bowl, flake the tuna and add the soy sauce and mirin. Transfer to a small container and refrigerate, tightly closed, for at least 4 hours or overnight.

Put the celery in a small, heatproof bowl. In a small saucepan, combine the vinegar, sugar, salt, and 1 Tbsp of water, and warm over low heat until the liquid is steaming and the sugar has dissolved. Pour over the celery and let cool to room temperature. Transfer to another small container and refrigerate, tightly covered, for at least 1 hour or overnight.

When you're ready to make the sandwiches, put the red onion in a small bowl of ice water to soak while you prepare the rest of the ingredients. This step is optional, but it will neutralize the onion's astringent bite, leaving the onion sweet and crisp.

Drain both the tuna mix and the pickled celery thoroughly. Combine them in a medium bowl, add 2 Tbsp of the Kewpie mayo, and stir to combine. Set aside.

In a small bowl, mix the remaining 2 Tbsp of mayo with the ao nori and yuzu kosho. Spread it evenly across all four slices of bread. Tile the cucumber rounds across the surface of each bread slice. Divide the tuna salad between two of the slices, carefully distributing it to the edges. Pat the onions dry on a paper towel and sprinkle them across the surface of the tuna. Place the remaining 2 slices of bread on top. Cut off the crusts, cut each sandwich into thirds lengthwise, and serve immediately.

Triple Pickle Smoked Salmon Butter Sandwich

Like many New Yorkers, I fell in love with focaccia sandwiches at Saltie, a small sandwich shop in Williamsburg, now closed. Saltie tucked ribbons of mortadella, piles of pickles, and smatterings of herbs into bubbly, golden brown squares of fresh focaccia. The bread is surprisingly sturdy, and a wide slice does a great job of containing small, crunchy sandwich toppings. This sandwich combines smoked salmon butter, pickled shallots, Turmeric-Pickled Cauliflower (page 46), and Beet-Pickled Eggs (page 120) for a veritable sunset of flavors and textures, all brightened with a sprinkling of crisp herbs. The smoked salmon butter creates a barrier across the bottom half of the focaccia, which prevents the bread from getting soggy. Which means it's a great candidate for taking to the park for a twilight picnic.

ONE 3½ OZ [100 G] TIN SMOKED SALMON

3 TBSP SALTED BUTTER, AT ROOM TEMPERATURE

1 TBSP PICKLED SHALLOTS (PAGE 44)

FRESHLY GROUND BLACK PEPPER

TWO 5 IN [13 CM] SQUARES FOCACCIA

⅓ CUP [50 G] TURMERIC-PICKLED CAULIFLOWER (PAGE 46), COARSELY CHOPPED

1 BEET-PICKLED EGG (PAGE 120), THINLY SLICED

½ CUP [7 G] PERFECTLY DRESSED HERB SALAD (PAGE 57)

Makes 2 sandwiches In a small bowl, mash the salmon with the butter and pickled shallots. Season with black pepper. Cut each focaccia square in half horizontally, leaving the halves attached at a hinge, like a hamburger bun. Spread the salmon butter across the bottom cut surface of each square of focaccia.

Sprinkle the cauliflower over the butter and distribute the egg slices between the two sandwiches. Sprinkle the herb salad on top. Close the sandwiches and serve or wrap in wax paper if you're taking these on a picnic.

Sardine Banh Mi

RECIPE BY
ANDREA NGUYEN

I'll happily eat any baguette that's stuffed with meaty sardines, but add some mayo, pickled daikon, carrot, and plenty of fresh, peppery cilantro, and now we're really talking. As author Andrea Nguyen explains in her 2014 cookbook, *The Banh Mi Handbook*, the combination hearkens back to the first half of the twentieth century, when French colonialism introduced tinned ingredients like sardines to Vietnamese cuisine. Whether packed in oil or tomato sauce, the fish are a satisfying sandwich filling straight from the can, but this recipe borrows a technique from Andrea's grandmother: bringing the tomato sauce to life with fried shallots, a touch of ketchup for sweetness, and some fresh lime juice. Like any great banh mi, this one is pulled together with mayo that's been sprinkled with Maggi seasoning, a salty, concentrated sauce that brings out the sandwich's savory undertones.

DAIKON AND CARROT PICKLE

ONE 4 IN [10 CM] LENGTH DAIKON, PEELED AND JULIENNED

1 MEDIUM CARROT, PEELED AND JULIENNED

½ TSP KOSHER SALT

1 TSP PLUS ¼ CUP [50 G] SUGAR

½ CUP [120 ML] DISTILLED WHITE VINEGAR

SANDWICH

ONE 4 OZ [115 G] CAN SARDINES IN TOMATO SAUCE, UNDRAINED

1 TBSP CANOLA OIL

1 SMALL SHALLOT, MINCED

1½ TSP KETCHUP

1 TSP FRESH LIME JUICE

½ BAGUETTE OR 2 BOLILLO ROLLS

2 TBSP MAYONNAISE

7 OR 8 DROPS MAGGI SEASONING

½ JALAPEÑO PEPPER, CUT INTO THIN ROUNDS

1 PERSIAN CUCUMBER, CUT INTO LONG, THIN BATONS

3 OR 4 SPRIGS FRESH CILANTRO

con't

Makes 2 sandwiches   TO MAKE THE PICKLE: In a small bowl, massage the daikon and carrot with the salt and 1 tsp of the sugar for about 3 minutes, or until the vegetables are flexible and have shed some of their water. Transfer to a mesh strainer and rinse with cold water. Transfer the daikon and carrot to a 1 pt [475 ml] container and add the remaining ¼ cup [50 g] of sugar, the vinegar, and ½ cup [120 ml] of water. Stir to dissolve the sugar, cover, and refrigerate for at least 1 hour.

TO MAKE THE SANDWICHES: Transfer the sardines to a small bowl, leaving the tomato sauce in the can. In a small skillet over medium-high heat, warm the canola oil and add the shallot. Fry for about 4 minutes until the shallot starts to brown.

Remove from the heat, and stir in the tomato sauce from the can, the ketchup, and the lime juice. Over low heat, simmer for 3 to 4 minutes, until the flavors have married and the liquid has reduced slightly. Add the sardines and use a spatula to break them into a few large pieces. Cook for about 1 minute more, until the fish is warmed through.

Cut the baguette half into two 6 in [15 cm] lengths, and cut each one through the side lengthwise, leaving a hinge, so the tops and bottoms are still connected. Spread mayonnaise across the surface of all four cut sides and sprinkle the Maggi seasoning over the mayo. Scatter the sardine pieces over the bottom halves of the sandwiches, and top with the carrot and daikon pickle, sliced jalapeño, cucumber, and cilantro. Serve immediately.

The Ultimate Beach Sub

One of the great joys of summer in Brooklyn is hopping on a bus, train, or bike, and in less than an hour, finding yourself on a public beach. The experience is even better if you happen to pick up a few Italian sandwiches on the way (Defonte's and Brancaccio's are two of my go-tos). This sandwich is an ode to the Italian tuna sub—full of creamy tuna salad, delicately sliced red onion, hot peppers, and crisp iceberg lettuce tossed with Italian dressing.

1 TSP OLIVE OIL

1 TSP RED WINE VINEGAR

½ TSP SUGAR

½ SMALL GARLIC CLOVE, GRATED

PINCH OF DRIED OREGANO

FRESHLY GROUND BLACK PEPPER

¼ RED ONION

ONE 5 OZ [140 G] CAN TUNA IN OLIVE OIL, DRAINED

1 CELERY STALK, MINCED

2 TBSP MAYONNAISE

½ BEEFSTEAK TOMATO

PINCH OF KOSHER SALT

¼ HEAD ICEBERG LETTUCE, THINLY SHREDDED

1 LONG, THIN LOAF CRUSTY ITALIAN BREAD OR BAGUETTE

¼ CUP [25 G] HOT PICKLED PEPPER RINGS OR SLICED PICKLED BANANA PEPPERS

Makes 2 sandwiches   Start by making the Italian dressing. In a small bowl, whisk together the olive oil, vinegar, sugar, garlic, oregano, and a few grinds of pepper. Let sit so that the garlic infuses the liquid and the sugar dissolves.

Cut the ¼ of a red onion in half. Mince one chunk and transfer to a small bowl. Thinly slice the other and set aside. Add the tuna to the small bowl with the minced onion, and then the celery, mayonnaise, and a few grinds of black pepper, and mix with a fork until the tuna has broken into very small flakes and everything is well incorporated.

con't

Thinly slice the tomato and cut the slices into half moons. Set the tomato slices on a paper towel and sprinkle with the kosher salt. This will both season the tomatoes and draw out any excess water, so your sandwich doesn't get soggy.

In a third small bowl, toss the lettuce with the thinly sliced red onion and the Italian dressing.

Cut two 8 in [20 cm] long pieces off the loaf of bread and save the rest for another use. Cut each piece of bread through the side lengthwise, leaving a hinge, so the tops and bottoms are still connected. Spread them open on a clean, dry work surface. Divide the tomato slices between the bottom halves of the bread. Top with the tuna salad, and then the peppers, and finally the lettuce.

Close the sandwiches and press the top lightly as you cut each one in half. Serve immediately or wrap tightly in wax paper to take to the beach.

THE PERFECT TUNA SALAD ANYTIME, ANYWHERE

Following a precise recipe for tuna salad may feel a little silly. After all, the mix is often a way to make a really awesome sandwich out of whatever's in your refrigerator and pantry. Some of the best tuna sandwiches I've made were a result of a miscellany of pickled things and fresh herbs from my refrigerator. Onion and celery may be standard, but sometimes you're in the mood for green onions and tarragon, or pepperoncini and shallots, or capers and dill. Here's a formula to transform that tin into something delicious, whether you're making lunch at home, in a sparsely stocked friend's kitchen, or at an unfamiliar rental house.

SOMETHING FROM A TIN

Start with one 5 oz [140 g] can of fish. I often prefer tuna packed in olive oil, but since you're going to be mixing it with something rich and creamy, you can also get away with solid tuna packed in water. You can even try this with another flaky, meaty fish, like mackerel. Species doesn't matter terribly much here—just choose something you enjoy. Drain the can and put the meat in a medium bowl, using a fork to break it into small flakes.

SOMETHING CREAMY

Use about 2 Tbsp. My go-to here is a classic store-bought mayo, but there are plenty of possibilities. This is a great opportunity to use leftover homemade aioli. For an extra umami boost, you can opt for Kewpie mayo, which LA's Konbi uses in their Tuna Fish Sandwich (page 147). Or, to keep the flavors bright and tangy, try a little crème fraîche here.

SOMETHING ONIONY

Aim for about 2 Tbsp of white onion, shallots, green onions, or ramps to add a soft allium bite to the salad. A fine mince is key, so the flavor is distributed throughout the tuna salad.

SOMETHING CRUNCHY, BRINY, OR HERBY

Here's where you can get really adventurous. Mix in 2 Tbsp of finely chopped crunchy vegetables, pickled things, or fresh herbs. In addition to the usual celery, this is a great time to use a few cornichons or capers, pickled banana peppers, or pepperoncini. Dill, tarragon, and parsley will add freshness and some much-needed green.

TASTE AND SEASON

Before the salad makes its way onto your sandwich, mix it well, and give it a taste for seasoning. The canned tuna, mayo, and any pickles you added might already have you covered on the salty front, but a few grinds of black pepper can go a long way. If your salad leans more on alliums, herbs, and fresh vegetables than it does on briny things, then you might want to add a few drops of white wine vinegar for a touch of acidity.

The Tuna Melt

A few years ago, joined by a small group of fellow tinned fish enthusiasts, I went on a tuna melt crawl through Lower Manhattan. (It sounds crazy, I know.) We started at Kossar's for a petite, round bialy melt, and then made our way to Odessa, B&H Dairy, and Eisenberg's. And though it's counterintuitive, with each tuna melt I consumed, I grew more and more hungry for the next one.

To me, the tuna melt is one of the most perfect sandwiches in existence—simple enough that you could eat six of them in a day without getting tired of them, but adaptable enough that diners and home cooks can add their own touch. This recipe is my celebration of the sandwich's toastiest, cheesiest, creamiest, and crunchiest qualities.

ONE 5 OZ [140 G] CAN TUNA IN OLIVE OIL, DRAINED

2 TBSP MAYONNAISE

1 CELERY STALK, MINCED

1 GREEN ONION (WHITE AND GREEN PARTS), MINCED

1 TBSP PICKLED SHALLOTS (PAGE 44)

FRESHLY GROUND BLACK PEPPER

KOSHER SALT (OPTIONAL)

2 TBSP BUTTER

4 THIN SLICES SHARP YELLOW CHEDDAR CHEESE

4 SLICES MARBLE RYE

Makes 2 sandwiches In a small bowl, use a fork to mix the tuna with the mayonnaise, celery, green onion, and shallots. Add a few grinds of pepper, taste for seasoning, and add salt if needed.

In a large skillet, heat 1½ Tbsp of the butter over medium heat. Lay out two slices of rye. Place a slice of cheese on each one. Top with the tuna, followed by the remaining cheddar, and the remaining slices of rye.

Carefully transfer the sandwiches to the skillet, and cook for about 4 minutes, until the bottom of the sandwich has browned and the cheese has melted slightly. Add the remaining 1½ tsp of butter to the skillet, carefully flip the sandwiches (using two spatulas if needed), and cover the skillet. Cook for 4 more minutes, or until both sides are browned and the cheese has completely melted. Serve immediately.

5

THE MAIN ATTRACTIONS

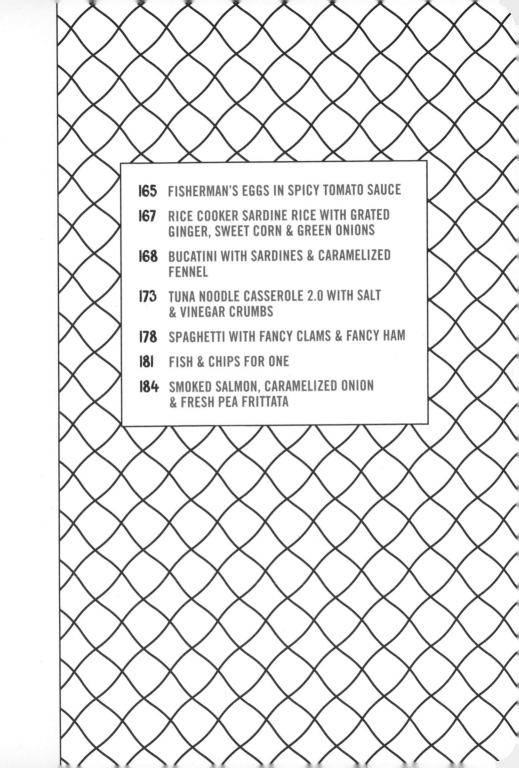

Tinned fish may be a pantry item, but like any other meat or seafood, you can build a meal around it. If you don't want to blow through that pricey tin of cockles during cocktail hour, turn them into a sophisticated spaghetti dish that tastes like the sea, and punctuate it with crispy petals of prosciutto. Need an easy spring brunch centerpiece? Make a smoked salmon frittata with fresh peas and caramelized onions, and serve it with a crusty baguette.

The recipes in this chapter have you covered, whether you're stuck at home craving pub fare, in the mood for a gutsy pasta, or just looking for a satisfying, protein-packed way to feed yourself during a busy workday.

Fisherman's Eggs in Spicy Tomato Sauce

The concept behind fisherman's eggs is simple: Cook a few sardines quickly in a skillet, along with onions, parsley, and whatever else you have lying around. Then crack a few eggs into the skillet. It's not a recipe as much as a model for how to turn a few grocery items you already have on hand into a warm, hearty meal. In my version, the sardines are cooked in a Calabrian chili and garlic–packed tomato sauce, into which the eggs are dropped, like a shakshuka. After about 20 minutes, you'll have a one-pot dinner. You can even skip the utensils, if you have half a baguette to dip right into the skillet.

2 TBSP OLIVE OIL

1 SMALL SHALLOT, MINCED

4 GARLIC CLOVES, MINCED

1 TSP CALABRIAN CHILI PASTE, OR A LARGE PINCH OF RED PEPPER FLAKES

¼ TSP KOSHER SALT

ONE 14½ OZ [410 G] CAN CRUSHED TOMATOES

ONE 4 TO 5 OZ [115 TO 140 G] CAN SARDINES IN OLIVE OIL, DRAINED

4 EGGS

2 TBSP MINCED FRESH FLAT-LEAF PARSLEY

CRUSTY BREAD, FOR SERVING

Serves 2   In a small Dutch oven (or a medium sauté pan with a lid) over medium-low heat, warm the olive oil. Add the shallot, garlic, chili paste, and salt, and cook for 3 minutes, stirring frequently. Add the crushed tomatoes and bring to a simmer. Cook for 12 minutes, or until the liquid from the tomatoes has reduced slightly and the tomatoes are infused with the flavors of the aromatics. Add the sardines and break each fish into bite-size pieces with your spoon or spatula.

With the back of a spoon, make four indentations in the tomato sauce. Crack an egg into each one and cover the pot. Lower the heat to low and cook for about 3 minutes, or until the egg whites are just set. Sprinkle with the parsley and serve immediately with the bread.

Rice Cooker Sardine Rice

with Grated Ginger, Sweet Corn & Green Onions

RECIPE BY
NAOKO
TAKEI MOORE

After interviewing Naoko Takei Moore for *TASTE* a few years ago, I became a quick convert to cooking with donabe, clay pots that have been part of Japan's culinary history for centuries. Naoko's business, TOIRO, sells a variety of donabe, and her book, *Donabe*, shares some of the joys and rituals of preparing and sharing meals in clay.

One of the first dishes I cooked with my kamado-san (rice cooker) donabe was one that Naoko posted on Instagram—a fluffy bed of rice cooked in dashi, soy sauce, and sake, under a sunburst of tiny silver sardines. The sardine oil coats each grain of rice, seasoning it and creating a toasty golden crust where it meets the clay surface. This adaptation, with sweet corn and a whisper of shiso, is designed for an electric rice cooker. But if you enjoy it, I encourage you to pick up a donabe of your own.

---

1 CUP [200 G] SHORT-GRAIN WHITE RICE

¾ CUP [180 ML] PLUS 2 TBSP CHICKEN STOCK, DASHI, OR WATER

ONE 1 IN [2.5 CM] PIECE FRESH GINGER, PEELED AND JULIENNED

2 TBSP SOY SAUCE

1 EAR FRESH CORN, HUSKED AND KERNELS CUT OFF THE COB

ONE 3¾ OZ [105 G] TIN SMALL SARDINES IN OLIVE OIL (SUCH AS KING OSCAR TINY TOTS), UNDRAINED

4 FRESH SHISO LEAVES, CUT INTO A CHIFFONADE

3 GREEN ONIONS (GREEN PART ONLY), THINLY SLICED

Serves 2   Rinse the rice under cold running water until the water runs clear. Drain thoroughly and transfer to the rice cooker. Add the stock, ginger, soy sauce, and corn kernels. Give the rice cooker a gentle shake to mix everything.

Very carefully, with your hands or a pair of chopsticks, arrange the sardines in a circle around the perimeter of the rice cooker, tails pointing toward the center. Drizzle the oil from the sardine can into the rice cooker and cover. Cook according to your rice cooker instructions, on the setting you would typically use for white rice.

Once the rice is cooked, use the rice paddle to fluff the rice and break up the sardines, incorporating them throughout. Garnish with the shiso and green onions, and serve.

Bucatini with Sardines & Caramelized Fennel

This is sort of a simplified version of pasta con le sarde, a Sicilian dish that blends fennel and sardines with a flurry of other pantry ingredients, spinning any old tin of sardines into a pasta that would be worth traveling for. Some versions include pine nuts, capers, and currants. I personally like the sweetness of yellow raisins, and if you chop them before adding, their subtle sweetness will be distributed throughout the dish. I also like to double down on the flavors and textures of fennel, mincing some to cook with the onions and garlic, caramelizing a few wedges, and topping the whole thing with fennel seed–flavored bread crumbs and plenty of lacy green fronds.

KOSHER SALT

3 TBSP OLIVE OIL

2 ANCHOVY FILLETS, MINCED

¼ CUP [15 G] PANKO

¼ TSP FENNEL SEEDS

1 LARGE FENNEL BULB, ROOT END TRIMMED AND FRONDS TRIMMED AND RESERVED

1 SMALL YELLOW ONION, CHOPPED

4 GARLIC CLOVES, MINCED

¼ CUP [35 G] YELLOW RAISINS, COARSELY CHOPPED

¼ CUP [60 ML] WHITE WINE

1 LB [455 G] BUCATINI

TWO 3 TO 4 OZ [85 TO 115 G] CANS SARDINES IN OLIVE OIL, DRAINED

Serves 4   Fill a large pot with water, add a big pinch of salt, and bring to a boil.

In a large skillet, heat 1 Tbsp of the olive oil over medium-low heat. Add the anchovies and stir until they begin to break down and dissolve into the oil. Stir in the panko and fennel seeds. Cook, stirring, for about 4 minutes, until the bread crumbs turn light brown. Remove from the heat, and use a spatula or slotted spoon to transfer the bread crumb mixture to a small bowl. Set aside.

Wash a big handful of the fennel fronds and wrap gently in a dish towel to dry. Coarsely chop and set aside.

con't

Remove the outer three or four layers of the fennel bulb and mince. You should be left with a small bulb—about half the weight of the original. Cut into eight wedges.

Return the skillet to medium-low heat and add 1 Tbsp of the olive oil. Place the fennel wedges gently in the pan, sprinkle with a pinch of salt, and cook for 5 minutes, or until they're golden brown on the bottom. Use tongs to flip and cook for 5 minutes on the other side. Transfer to a small plate.

Add the remaining 1 Tbsp of olive oil to the skillet, still over medium-low heat, and add the minced fennel, onion, garlic, and raisins. Cook, stirring, for about 4 minutes, until the onion and fennel have softened and the garlic has become fragrant. Add the white wine and cook for 2 minutes more. Remove from the heat.

Cook the bucatini in the boiling water according to the instructions on the package until al dente (usually 1 minute less than the recommended time). Drain, reserving ¼ cup [60 ml] of the cooking water.

Return the skillet to medium-high heat and add the pasta and the reserved cooking water. Cook, using tongs to toss the pasta with the aromatics, until the water evaporates and the pasta is perfectly done. Break the sardines apart with your fingers and add them to the skillet. Toss them with the pasta until just heated through and remove the skillet from the heat.

Toss half the fennel fronds and half the bread crumbs into the pasta and divide among four plates. Top with the caramelized fennel wedges and the remaining fennel fronds and bread crumbs.

THE FRENCH ART OF AGING SARDINES

Just like grapes, there are good years and bad years for sardine harvests. And just like wine, there's a whole world of sardine enthusiasts out there who collect their cans by the vintage on the label and even age these fish to improve their quality since some extra time in the tin can tenderize the meat, allowing it to gradually soak up the oil.

While sardines are generally safe to eat for years past their "best by" dates, as long as the can hasn't been damaged, most collectors agree that the best ones to age for more than a couple years are the ones packed in olive oil, with no acidic ingredients or other flavorings. And as Margaret Costa writes in her famous 1970 book, *Four Seasons Cookery Book*, "Like wines, if sardines are good in the first place, they are worth laying down."

Following this principle, several sardine producers, like Rödel and Connétable in France, print vintage dates on their premium cans. Zingerman's, a deli and specialty food store in Ann Arbor, Michigan, even sells curated boxes of sardines from some of their favorite vintages of the past decade.

Seek out some of these to get your collection started, and keep them in a cool, dark place, rotating the cans from time to time to ensure that the fish remain coated evenly in liquid. The next time you need a can to pop open for a special occasion, you'll know where to find it.

Tuna Noodle Casserole 2.0
with Salt & Vinegar Crumbs

Tuna noodle casserole gets a lot of guff, and I'm going to be honest—I sort of get it. The versions a lot of us had as kids often consisted of overcooked egg noodles, made even soggier by canned cream of mushroom soup, barely seasoned. But if you're a tuna noodle skeptic, I'm here to change your mind. In this version, I swap in al dente cavatappi ("corkscrews") in place of the limp egg noodles, and a peppery mushroom-infused béchamel stands in for the soup. Green onions add some fresh high notes over the mellow undertones of yellow onion and celery, and the whole thing is topped with a buttery mix of panko and crushed salt and vinegar potato chips, which get toasty in the oven. The effect is a casserole that satisfies all your kitschy cravings, with a few modern innovations.

KOSHER SALT

1 LB [455 G] CAVATAPPI OR SIMILAR SPIRAL-SHAPED PASTA

5 TBSP [75 G] BUTTER

¾ CUP [45 G] PANKO

¾ CUP [55 G] CRUSHED SALT AND VINEGAR POTATO CHIPS

1 MEDIUM YELLOW ONION, DICED

1 CELERY STALK, DICED

10 OZ [285 G] CREMINI MUSHROOMS, STEMS TRIMMED AND CAPS THINLY SLICED

¼ CUP [60 ML] WHITE WINE OR DRY VERMOUTH

¼ CUP [35 G] ALL-PURPOSE FLOUR

3 CUPS [710 ML] WHOLE MILK

FRESHLY GROUND BLACK PEPPER

TWO 5 OZ [140 G] CANS TUNA IN OLIVE OIL OR WATER, DRAINED

1 BUNCH GREEN ONIONS (GREEN PART ONLY), THINLY SLICED

8 OZ [230 G] FROZEN PETITE PEAS

con't

Serves 4 to 6   Preheat the oven to 375°F [190°C].
Butter a 9 by 13 in [23 by 33 cm] casserole dish or
lasagna pan.

Fill a large pot with water, add a big pinch of salt,
and bring to a boil. Add the cavatappi and cook for
6 minutes, or 1 minute short of al dente, and drain.
Meanwhile, melt 1 Tbsp of the butter in a small saucepan, remove from the heat, and stir in the panko and
potato chips. Set aside.

In a large Dutch oven over medium heat, melt 2 Tbsp of
the butter, and add the onion, celery, mushrooms, and
a pinch of salt. Cook for about 8 minutes, stirring regu-
larly. When their liquid has cooked off and the mushrooms begin to brown, add the wine. Cook for 2 minutes,
scraping the brown bits from the bottom of the pan.

Add the remaining 2 Tbsp of butter to the pot and
sprinkle the flour evenly over the mixture. Cook the
flour and vegetables in the butter for about 2 minutes,
or until the flour begins to brown and stick to the
bottom of the pot. Stir in the milk. Bring to a simmer
and cook, stirring constantly, for about 5 to 7 minutes,
or until the sauce thickens significantly. Remove
from the heat, and season with salt and black pepper.

Add the tuna to the Dutch oven and use a spatula
to break it into small pieces. Add the pasta, green
onions, and frozen peas, and toss everything with
the béchamel sauce. Pour the pasta mixture into the
baking dish, packing it down gently with the back of a
spatula. Sprinkle the panko and potato chip mixture
across the top. Bake for 20 minutes, or until the topping is golden brown, and serve immediately.

THE ART OF SALT-PACKING

Unlike most canned tuna and sardines, the salty brown anchovies we buy in little oval cans have been through a whole aging and curing process before they even reach the tin. Anchovies, freshly fished from the ocean, are beheaded and piled into large, round crocks, with handfuls of rock salt sprinkled between each layer of silvery fish.

Over the course of the next five to six months, the salt draws much of the moisture from the fish, creating a murky, pinkish liquid. Meanwhile, the anchovies cure, which turns their flesh from white to a deep reddish amber color and suffuses the meat with enough salty umami that each fillet could season a whole pot of sauce. The salt-curing process also acts as a means of partial preservation, keeping the uncooked fish edible for many months. Once the curing process is complete, the anchovies are rinsed, filleted, trimmed of their tails and fins, and packed into tins with olive oil. This is the form of anchovy you'll find at most American grocery stores.

A few legacy canning companies, like Ortiz and Agostina Recca, sell birthday cake–sized tins of salt-packed anchovies, which you can clean and fillet at home. While this approach takes a little work, you can add your own personal touch at the marinating stage, using that really delicious olive oil you brought back from your trip to Tuscany, or adding a few pinches of fruity chili flakes or thinly sliced garlic.

HOW TO CLEAN AND FILLET SALT-PACKED ANCHOVIES AT HOME

1. The first thing to remember about buying salt-packed anchovies is that you're buying a semipreserved product. This means that you should store it (even the unopened tin) in the refrigerator, and plan to begin using it within about 2 or 3 months of purchasing.

2. When you're ready to eat or cook with some anchovies, go ahead and crack that can open. If it looks a little scary, don't panic. Depending on how much time has passed between when the fish went into the can and when you're opening it, you might see salt caked over the fish, or the fish might be surrounded by a cloudy liquid. Prepare a bowl of cold water, and very carefully, with clean hands, remove as many fish as you want to eat or have handy for the coming week.

3. Gently rinse each fish under cold running water and put it in the bowl of cold water. Let soak for 15 minutes. This will draw out some of the excess salt from the fish and soften the meat slightly. In the meantime, set a few layers of paper towels across a cutting board. Remove the fish from the water and set them on the paper towels to drain.

4. Now comes the fun part— the filleting. Working on one fish at a time, gently pinch the flesh around the tail, wedging your thumb between the meat and the spine beneath it. Use your other hand to pin the tail down on the cutting board while you gently pull the flesh off the spine. Now pinch the spine, starting at the tail end, and lift it away from the bottom fillet.

5. Once the fillets are removed from the fish, you'll just want to make sure they're squeaky clean, with no guts or fins. Run your finger gently along the top and bottom of the fillet to feel for any hidden fins, which you can pull away, along with any mushy pieces of skin or viscera attached to the meat (it's okay for a bit of silvery skin to still be intact).

6. Give the fillets another quick rinse and lay them out on clean paper towels. Top with another layer of paper towels. Pat the fillets dry of excess moisture so they will last longer, with better flavor, in the refrigerator.

7. At this stage, the fillets are ready to be cooked. Or you can transfer them to a jar, cover them with olive oil, and cover the jar tightly with its lid. The anchovies will keep for 2 weeks, but I find they taste best and are freshest during the first 3 to 4 days.

8. Any remaining anchovies, which you haven't cleaned and filleted, can be kept in their original tin in the refrigerator for an additional 1 or 2 months. Just add enough kosher salt to the tin so that any exposed fish are covered, and wrap with a few tight layers of plastic wrap.

Spaghetti
with Fancy Clams & Fancy Ham

When I was between the ages of eight and twelve, one of my favorite meals was the pasta with white clam sauce my dad would make on the nights when just the two of us were home (presumably because none of my siblings were quite as excited by the prospect of canned clams as I was). This recipe hits quite a few of the same notes, marrying the clam brine with white wine and garlic. But it's zhuzhed up with delicate cockles and a sprinkling of pan-crisped prosciutto. The cockles are much more tender and sweet than most canned clams, and by adding them right at the end, you can preserve all of that texture and flavor without the risk of turning them rubbery. This is the pantry pasta to make when the pantry is stocked with the good stuff.

KOSHER SALT

2 TBSP OLIVE OIL

4 SLICES PROSCIUTTO, SERRANO HAM, OR COUNTRY HAM

2 LARGE GARLIC CLOVES, MINCED

¼ CUP [60 ML] DRY VERMOUTH OR WHITE WINE

ONE 4 OZ [115 G] CAN COCKLES IN BRINE, UNDRAINED

8 OZ [230 G] SPAGHETTI

2 TBSP MINCED FRESH FLAT-LEAF PARSLEY

1 TBSP FRESH LEMON JUICE

FRESHLY GROUND BLACK PEPPER

Serves 2 Fill a large pot with water, add a big pinch of salt, and bring to a rolling boil.

Meanwhile, add 1 Tbsp of the olive oil to a large skillet over medium-low heat. Spread out the slices of prosciutto in the skillet so they're not overlapping. Cook for 1½ to 2 minutes, and then use a pair of tongs to flip them over. Cook for about 1 minute more, until the slices have wrinkled, curled, and shrunken slightly. They should be a little bit crisp and will become more brittle as they cool. Transfer to a paper towel–lined plate.

con't

Add the remaining 1 Tbsp of olive oil and return the pan to medium-low heat. Add the garlic and shake the pan gently to move it around in the oil. Cook for about 2 minutes, until fragrant. Add the vermouth and shake the pan again gently. Cook for 2 minutes, or until reduced slightly.

Drain the brine from the can of cockles into the skillet. Simmer for 4 to 5 minutes, until slightly reduced, and remove from the heat. Set aside.

Cook the spaghetti in the boiling water according to the instructions on the package until al dente. Drain, reserving 2 Tbsp of the cooking water.

Return the brine and vermouth mixture to a simmer, and add the spaghetti and the reserved 2 Tbsp of cooking water. Toss the spaghetti with the liquid in the pan for about 4 minutes, until most of the liquid is absorbed and the pasta looks glossy. Remove from the heat.

Add the cockles, two-thirds of the parsley, and the lemon juice. Crumble 2 of the slices of prosciutto into the skillet and toss to combine. Season with salt and pepper. Divide the pasta between two bowls, and garnish with the remaining parsley and the remaining 2 slices of prosciutto. Serve immediately.

Fish & Chips for One

This is a dinner that puts all of my other low-on-groceries dinners to shame. If you have a single potato, a can of sardines, and a few more basic pantry ingredients, you are mere minutes away from a hearty (albeit slightly miniaturized) pub dinner. Since you want the sardines to stay intact through the battering and frying process, choose sardines with some good structure to them, and handle them as gently as possible. Bonus points if you find a couple of parsley sprigs in your refrigerator, so you can garnish the dish with the minced leaves, plus a wedge of lemon to serve alongside. But no judgment if your only accompaniment is a bottle of malt vinegar.

1 MEDIUM RUSSET POTATO

ONE 4 TO 5 OZ [115 TO 140 G] TIN SARDINES (MATIZ WORKS REALLY WELL HERE)

1 CUP [240 ML] VEGETABLE OIL

KOSHER SALT

¼ CUP [35 G] ALL-PURPOSE FLOUR

PINCH OF PAPRIKA

¼ CUP [60 ML] PLUS 1 TBSP UNFLAVORED COLD SELTZER

FRESHLY GROUND BLACK PEPPER

1 TSP MINCED FRESH FLAT-LEAF PARSLEY, FOR GARNISH (OPTIONAL)

1 LEMON WEDGE, FOR GARNISH (OPTIONAL)

Serves 1   Fill a small bowl with cold water. Cut the potato into ¼ in [6 mm] thick matchsticks and transfer to the bowl of water. Carefully remove the sardines from the tin and place on a paper towel–lined plate to blot the excess oil.

Line a baking sheet with paper towels. In a medium pot, heat the vegetable oil over medium heat until it reaches 350°F [180°C]. (If you don't have a thermometer, drop a tiny pinch of flour into the oil; if it makes a lot of small bubbles, then the oil is hot enough to fry.)

con't

Pat the potato sticks dry with a dish towel and add half of them to the oil. Fry for 5 minutes and use a slotted spoon to transfer them to the prepared baking sheet, spreading them out so that they don't stick together. Repeat with the remaining fries.

Once the second batch is out of the oil, return the first batch back to the oil and fry for an additional 5 minutes, or until they start to turn light brown, and transfer to the paper towel–lined baking sheet. Repeat with the remaining potato sticks. Sprinkle with a pinch of salt.

As your second batch is frying, in a small bowl, mix together the flour, paprika, and seltzer in a small bowl to create the batter. Season with salt and pepper.

Carefully dip each sardine into the batter and turn until it's fully coated. Slowly lower it into the pan, making sure your fingers don't touch the hot oil. Cook for 2 minutes and, with a slotted spoon, flip onto the opposite side to cook for 2 minutes more. Drain on a paper towel–lined plate.

Arrange the fish and fries on a plate, garnish with parsley and a lemon wedge, if desired, and eat while it's warm and crispy.

Smoked Salmon, Caramelized Onion & Fresh Pea Frittata

You might associate smoked salmon with the vacuum-packed, thinly sliced fillets that typically accompany a morning bagel. But smoked salmon in a tin can offers a world of breakfast possibilities. The best tinned salmon offers jewel-toned fillets infused with a rich cedar flavor, which work beautifully with a slice of toast and scrambled eggs, or in frittatas like this one, where the salmon teams up with caramelized onions and sweet, spring-like fresh peas. I like to serve this with some delicate greens or pea shoots dressed in olive oil and lemon juice, with a nice baguette.

4 EGGS

KOSHER SALT AND FRESHLY GROUND BLACK PEPPER

1 TBSP OLIVE OIL

1 MEDIUM YELLOW ONION, HALVED AND THINLY SLICED

1 TBSP BUTTER

½ CUP [85 G] FRESH SHELLED PEAS

ONE 3 TO 4 OZ [85 TO 115 G] TIN SMOKED SALMON

Serves 2 to 4   Crack the eggs into a medium bowl, season lightly with salt and pepper, and beat gently with a fork.

In a small skillet, heat the olive oil over medium heat, and add the onion. Cook, stirring constantly, for about 5 minutes, or until the onion begins to soften and turn translucent. Turn the heat as low as it will go and cover the skillet. Cook for 20 minutes, stirring every 5 to 7 minutes, until the onions become jammy in consistency. Uncover, return the heat to medium, and cook until the onions are evenly browned.

Stir in the butter, peas, and salmon, and use a spatula to gently break up the fillets into bite-size pieces. Pour the eggs evenly over the mixture. Cover the skillet and cook for 5 minutes. Turn the heat down to low, and cook for another 3 to 5 minutes, until the center is no longer jiggly. Season with more salt and pepper and serve.

VERY FUN PLACES TO SHOP FOR TINNED FISH

It's hard to think of a better souvenir than tins of fish. They're compact, the cans are often beautiful, and they give you a chance to look back wistfully while eating a really great sandwich or snack plate. I love the scavenger hunt involved in locating the best source for tins when I'm visiting a new city—it's a little like collecting mushrooms in *The Legend of Zelda: Breath of the Wild*.

But even if your travel is limited (as mine was while writing this book, thanks to COVID-19), there are plenty of online shops around the country and around the globe, each with its own character and style of curation. Here's a guide to some of my favorite spots for stocking up.

CAPUTO'S
Salt Lake City, UT
With free shipping in the United States on orders of over fifty dollars and more than a dozen brands of tinned fish from Spain, Portugal, France, and Denmark, Caputo's is a great place for fishy impulse purchases (and you might want to throw in a few chocolate bars while you're at it). *Caputos.com*

CONSERVA
online only
This chic online store sells an array of fancy tins, like Ramón Peña octopus and Conservas de Cambados sea urchin caviar, along with all the tableware and serving dishes for hosting a great party. *Conservaculture.com*

CUEVA NUEVA
online only
The Cueva Nueva Conservas Club offers a variety of quarterly subscription packages, depending on your level of adventurousness, your affection for bivalves, and the volume of tins you typically plow through in the course of a few months. *Cuevanueva.com*

DESPAÑA
New York, NY
With shops in two locations in metropolitan New York (Soho and Jackson Heights), Despaña is my go-to spot for Serrano ham, giant canisters of Bonilla a la Vista potato chips, paella rice, and plenty of Spanish tins from brands like Don Bocarte and Cabo de Peñas. *Despanabrandfoods.com*

HERMAN'S COFFEE
Philadelphia, PA
You can't walk into most neighborhood coffee shops and pick up a can of Gueyu Mar char-grilled cockles along with your cortado, but this is what makes Herman's Coffee, in South Philly, so special. *Hermanscoffee.square.sit*

LOJAS DAS CONSERVAS
Lisbon, Portugal
If you're on the fence about checking a bag on your way home from Lisbon, a trip to Lojas das Conservas will convince you that it's worthwhile. The shop is lined, floor to ceiling, with beautiful, ornate tins of sardines, tuna, and mackerel. *Lojadasconservas.com*

PORTUGALIA MARKETPLACE
Fall River, MA
The vast collection of tins will transport you straight to Lisbon. This is a great spot to find classic Portuguese brands like Nuri, Minerva, and Pinhais, but there are also plenty of brands that are harder to find stateside, like Cocagne, La Rose, and Minor.

Portugaliamarketplace.com

RAINBOW TOMATOES GARDEN
East Greenville, PA
In addition to growing hundreds of different types of tomatoes, Rainbow Tomatoes Garden boasts the largest collection of tinned seafood in the world, which can be viewed online. They ship to anywhere in the United States.

Rainbowtomatoesgarden.com

THE SHOP
Portland, ME
This outpost of Island Creek Oysters, a notable oyster farm in Duxbury, Massachusetts, is not only a great place to stop for a Bloody Mary and some fresh oysters—it's also a great place to stock up on sardines.

Shop.islandcreekoysters.com

TINCANFISH
online only
Because TinCanFish encourages bulk ordering (most products come in three-packs, six-packs, and twelve-packs), you'll find some remarkable prices here for your favorite tins, from Minerva and Porthos. If a twelve-pack of sardines in tomato sauce overwhelms you, the seasonal variety packs are also full of interesting treasures.

Tincanfish.com

TINMONGER
online only
This Canadian online retailer (with shipping across the United States and Canada) stocks lots of JOSE Gourmet and Yurrita products, but they were also the online shop to introduce me to Los Peperetes, a Galician brand that packages their spicy sardines, squid, goose barnacles, mussels, and cockles in stunning slim round tins. *Tinmonger.ca*

THE TINNED FISH MARKET
London, United Kingdom
Since the Tinned Fish Market is based in the United Kingdom, shipping to the United States can be pricey. But if you're an enthusiastic tin scavenger, it may be worth it for some of the brands that aren't typically imported into the United States, like Zallo and Splendida. The store also carries premium anchovies, like Olasagasti's "special selection" Cantabrian anchovies and Yurrita's beautiful butterflied anchovies.

Thetinnedfishmarket.com

ZINGERMAN'S DELI
Ann Arbor, MI
Ann Arbor's favorite specialty grocery and deli might be as well known for their tinned fish selection as for their legendary Reuben sandwich. Their tin selection includes lots of standards, some obscure picks, and a curated box of recent vintages.

Zingermans.com

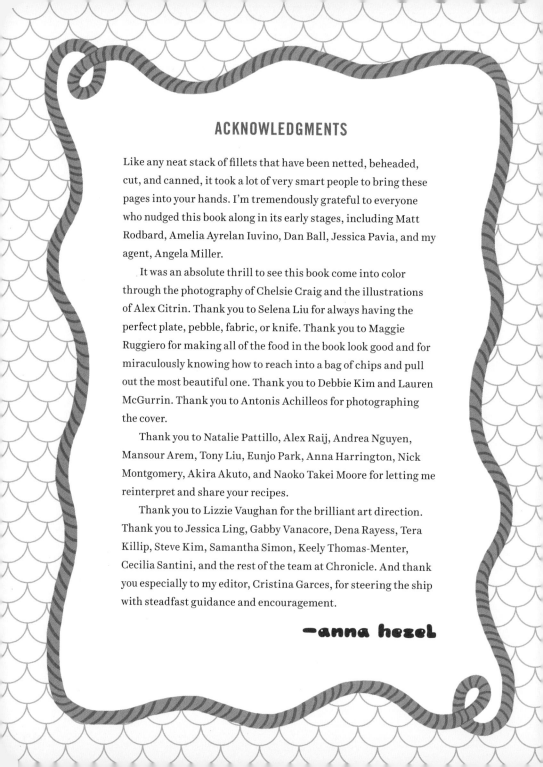

ACKNOWLEDGMENTS

Like any neat stack of fillets that have been netted, beheaded, cut, and canned, it took a lot of very smart people to bring these pages into your hands. I'm tremendously grateful to everyone who nudged this book along in its early stages, including Matt Rodbard, Amelia Ayrelan Iuvino, Dan Ball, Jessica Pavia, and my agent, Angela Miller.

It was an absolute thrill to see this book come into color through the photography of Chelsie Craig and the illustrations of Alex Citrin. Thank you to Selena Liu for always having the perfect plate, pebble, fabric, or knife. Thank you to Maggie Ruggiero for making all of the food in the book look good and for miraculously knowing how to reach into a bag of chips and pull out the most beautiful one. Thank you to Debbie Kim and Lauren McGurrin. Thank you to Antonis Achilleos for photographing the cover.

Thank you to Natalie Pattillo, Alex Raij, Andrea Nguyen, Mansour Arem, Tony Liu, Eunjo Park, Anna Harrington, Nick Montgomery, Akira Akuto, and Naoko Takei Moore for letting me reinterpret and share your recipes.

Thank you to Lizzie Vaughan for the brilliant art direction. Thank you to Jessica Ling, Gabby Vanacore, Dena Rayess, Tera Killip, Steve Kim, Samantha Simon, Keely Thomas-Menter, Cecilia Santini, and the rest of the team at Chronicle. And thank you especially to my editor, Cristina Garces, for steering the ship with steadfast guidance and encouragement.

—anna hezel

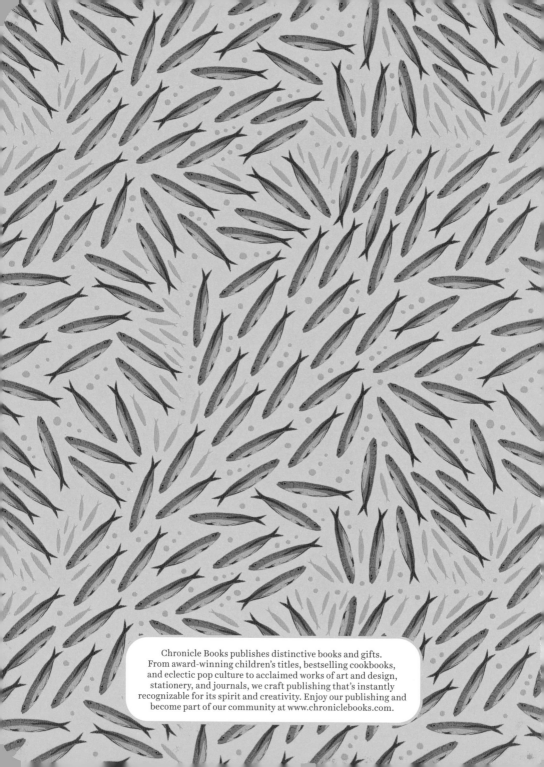

Chronicle Books publishes distinctive books and gifts.
From award-winning children's titles, bestselling cookbooks,
and eclectic pop culture to acclaimed works of art and design,
stationery, and journals, we craft publishing that's instantly
recognizable for its spirit and creativity. Enjoy our publishing and
become part of our community at www.chroniclebooks.com.